Editor
Stephanie Buehler, Psy.D.

Editorial Project Manager
Ina Massler Levin, M.A.

Editor in Chief
Sharon Coan, M.S. Ed.

Illustrator
Victoria Ponikvar-Frazier

Cover Artist
Jessica Orlando

Art Coordinator
Denice Adorno

Creative Director
Elayne Roberts

Imaging
Alfred Lau
Ralph Olmedo, Jr.

Product Manager
Phil Garcia

Publishers
Rachelle Cracchiolo, M.S. Ed.
Mary Dupuy Smith, M.S. Ed.

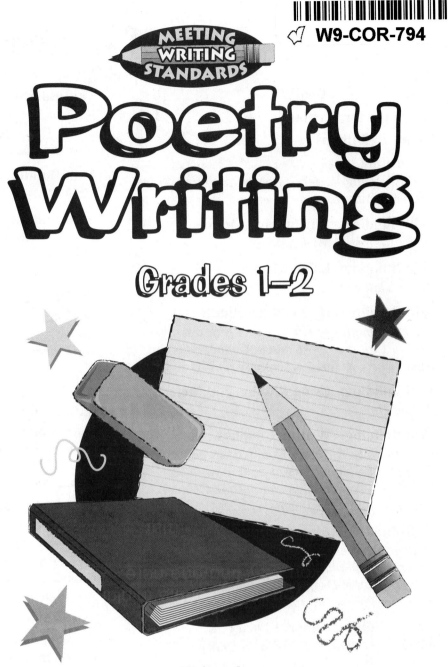

MEETING WRITING STANDARDS

Poetry Writing

Grades 1–2

Written by

Kathleen "Casey" Null

Teacher Created Materials, Inc.
6421 Industry Way
Westminster, CA 92683

www.teachercreated.com

ISBN-1-57690-984-0

©2000 Teacher Created Materials, Inc.
Made in U.S.A.

Table of Contents

How to Use this Book

Although young children may enjoy hearing and reading poetry, the idea of creating poetry may be intimidating for them. Before writing poetry, you may wish to read aloud to your students from collections of children's poetry and early readers that emphasize rhyme and rhythm.

Poetry Writing presents developmentally appropriate lessons that introduce students to various poems which they can create. The book begins with activities to generate ideas. Then there are 18 skill-building lessons which will allow students to master the standards on pages 4–6 while they learn to write some basic forms of poetry. Each lesson includes a definition of the genre, skills needed, if any, and materials to be gathered and prepared, including reproducible worksheets. The lessons lead students through each stage of the writing process and provide examples of student work as a guide. Feel free to modify the lessons for the ability level of your students. For example, pre-readers may need to dictate some poems, while capable readers can work independently.

For each poem that the students write, there is a response form for peer, self, and teacher evaluation. Each genre also includes Content Connections—activities that tie poetry writing to other subjects—that are designed to be copied, cut, and glued to 5" x 7" (13 cm x 18 cm) cards that can be kept in a file box in your writing center.

The students can create a poetry collection as a culminating activity. In this section, you will find reproducible worksheets that lead students through the process. If the facilities are available and the students capable, they may be encouraged to use computers in the creation of their collections. In any case, encourage creativity, color, and fun.

Standards for Writing
Grades K–2

Accompanying the major activities of this book will be references to the basic standards and benchmarks for writing that will be met by successful performance of the activities. Each specific standard and benchmark will be referred to by the appropriate letter and number from the following collection. For example, a basic standard and benchmark identified as **1A** would be as follows:

> **Standard 1:** Demonstrates competence in the general skills and strategies of the writing process
>
> **Benchmark A:** Prewriting: Uses prewriting strategies to plan written work (e.g., discusses ideas with peers, draws pictures to generate ideas, writes key thoughts and questions, rehearses ideas, records reactions and observations)

A standard and benchmark identified as **4B** would be as follows:

> **Standard 4:** Gathers and uses information for research purposes
>
> **Benchmark B:** Uses books to gather information for research topics (e.g., uses table of contents, examines pictures and charts)

Clearly, some activities will address more than one standard. Moreover, since there is a rich supply of activities included in this book, some will overlap in the skills they address, and some, of course, will not address every single benchmark within a given standard. Therefore, when you see these standards referenced in the activities, refer to this section for complete descriptions.

Although virtually every state has published its own standards and every subject area maintains its own lists, there is surprising commonality among these various sources. For the purposes of this book, we have elected to use the collection of standards synthesized by John S. Kendall and Robert J. Marzano in their book *Content Knowledge: A Compendium of Standards and Benchmarks for K–12 Education* (Second Edition, 1997) as illustrative of what students at various grade levels should know and be able to do. The book is published jointly by McRel (Mid-continent Regional Educational Laboratory, Inc.) and ASCD (Association for Supervision and Curriculum Development). (Used by permission of McRel.)

Language Arts Standards

1. Demonstrates competence in the general skills and strategies of the writing process

2. Demonstrates competence in the stylistic and rhetorical aspects of writing

3. Uses grammatical and mechanical conventions in written compositions

4. Gathers and uses information for research purposes

Standards for Writing
Grades K–2

---

1. Demonstrates competence in the general skills and strategies of the writing process

    A. Prewriting: Uses prewriting strategies to plan written work (e.g., discusses ideas with peers, draws pictures to generate ideas, writes key thoughts and questions, rehearses ideas, records reactions and observations)

    B. Drafting and Revising: Uses strategies to draft and revise written work (e.g., rereads; rearranges words, sentences, and paragraphs to improve or clarify meaning; varies sentence types; adds descriptive words and details; deletes extraneous information; incorporates suggestions from peers and teachers; sharpens the focus)

    C. Editing and Publishing: Uses strategies to edit and publish written work (e.g., proofreads using a dictionary and other resources; edits for grammar, punctuation, capitalization, and spelling at a developmentally appropriate level; incorporates illustrations or photos, shares finished product)

    D. Evaluates own and others' writing (e.g., asks questions and makes comments about writing, helps classmates apply grammatical and mechanical conventions)

    E. Dictates or writes with a logical sequence of events (e.g., includes a beginning, middle, and ending)

    F. Dictates or writes detailed descriptions of familiar persons, places, objects, or experiences

    G. Writes in response to literature

    H. Writes in a variety of formats (e.g., picture books, letters, stories, poems, and information pieces)

---

2. Demonstrates competence in the stylistic and rhetorical aspects of writing

    A. Uses general, frequently used words to convey basic ideas

Standards for Writing

Grades K–2

---

3. Uses grammatical and mechanical conventions in written compositions

   A. Forms letters in print and spaces words and sentences

   B. Uses complete sentences in written compositions

   C. Uses declarative and interrogative sentences in written compositions

   D. Uses nouns in written compositions (e.g., nouns for simple objects, family members, community workers, and categories)

   E. Uses verbs in written compositions (e.g., verbs for a variety of situations, action words)

   F. Uses adjectives in written compositions (e.g., uses descriptive words)

   G. Uses adverbs in written compositions (i.e., uses words that answer how, when, where, and why questions)

   H. Uses conventions of spelling in written compositions (e.g., spells high frequency, commonly misspelled words from appropriate grade-level list; uses a dictionary and other resources to spell words; spells own first and last name)

   I. Uses conventions of capitalization in written compositions (e.g., first and last names, first word of a sentence)

   J. Uses conventions of punctuation in written compositions (e.g., uses periods after declarative sentences, uses question marks after interrogative sentences, uses commas in a series)

---

4. Gathers and uses information for research purposes

   A. Generates questions about topics of personal interest

   B. Uses books to gather information for research topics (e.g., uses table of contents, examines pictures and charts)

Poetry Definitions

When students are familiar with terms related to poetry, they feel more certain about listening to, reading, and writing poetry. Teach pronunciation by breaking the terms into manageable syllables and discuss the terms often. Reinforce learning with colorful posters and flashcards of the terms.

---

alliteration: several words used together that have the same beginning sounds
(Examples: *bouncing baby bunnies, slithering slimy snakes*)

couplet: two lines of poetry that rhyme
(Example: *Humpty Dumpty sat on a wall/Humpty Dumpty had a great fall.*)

free verse: expressive poems that do not follow any rules or patterns except those which the poet uses
(Example: *Free verse/Is poetry without rhyme/And no form to hold it in/You are free to soar and create/Snapshots in the air.*)

imagery: a picture made of words
(Example: *The rippling river sliced a ribbon through the field.*)

metaphor: comparing two things as if they were the same without using the words *like* or *as*
(Example: *The kitten is a ball of white fluff.*)

meter: a pattern of words that gives poetry a toe-tapping rhythm, with stressed and unstressed syllables
(Example: *Peter, Peter, pumpkin eater/Had a wife and couldn't keep her;/Put her in a pumpkin shell/And there he kept her very well.*)

onomatopoeia: words that sound like what they describe
(Examples: *buzz, swish, zip, hiss, growl*)

rhyme: when two or more words have the same ending sound
(Example: *Twinkle, twinkle little star/How I wonder what you are/Up above the world so high/Like a diamond in the sky.*)

simile: comparing two things using the words *like* or *as*
(Example: *He's as jumpy as a grasshopper!*)

Generating Ideas: Brainstorming Posters

Background for the Teacher

Materials needed: 5–10 large poster boards, large marker, kitchen timer or stopwatch

Lesson Plan

1. Name a topic for students to brainstorm (see list of suggested topics below).

2. Teach students how to brainstorm. Tell them to call out ideas on the chosen topic when you are facing them and to pause while you write down the ideas. Remind them that nearly all ideas are fine ideas. They should keep generating ideas until the kitchen timer rings.

3. Prepare a piece of poster board by writing the topic at the top. Set the timer for 3–5 minutes. Write down the students' ideas. Repeat several times, using different topics.

4. Display the posters where students can refer to them for ideas and as a reminder of how to brainstorm.

Suggested Brainstorming Topics

1. favorite stuffed animal
2. things in nature that you like
3. what you like to eat for breakfast
4. favorite things to do on a Saturday
5. what you dream about
6. what you want to be when you grow up
7. why you like recess
8. your favorite books
9. what to do when it's raining
10. fun things to do in the summer

Generating Ideas: Poetry Jamboree

Background for the Teacher

Materials needed: Tent and Tree Patterns (page 10); multicolored copy paper; green, tan, or brown butcher paper for a bulletin board background; blue paper cut into a river shape; bulletin board letters for "Poetry Jamboree"; Velcro dots (optional)

Preparation: Copy the patterns from Tent and Tree Patterns (page 10) as described in the directions on the page. Label the tents with the suggestions below.

Lesson Presentation

1. Place the background color on the bulletin board and add the paper river and trees.

2. Staple the paper tents to the background. If you wish, Velcro dots may be used instead so that each student can remove a tent to use at his or her desk.

3. Point out the bulletin board to students and explain that a jamboree is a large camp-out where ideas are exchanged and learning and sharing takes place. Instruct students in ways that they can use the Poetry Jamboree to generate new topics for poems.

Topics for the Poetry Jamboree Tents

• beach balls	• balloons	• crying
• dandelions	• babies	• wagons
• picture books	• socks	• jewelry
• music	• apples	• laughing
• rainbows	• toys	• tickling
• airplanes	• baseball	• fish
• licorice	• worms	• mud
• clouds	• rain	• baths
• ice cream	• giggling	• pictures
• kites	• dirt	• ants
• peanut butter	• crayons	• vegetables
• big brothers	• toothpaste	• flowers
• kittens	• bicycles	• toes
• big sisters	• mud pies	

Tent and Tree Patterns

Copy the tent patterns on light blue, orange, light orange, light green, and yellow construction paper. Write the suggested topics (page 9) on the tents, cut them out, and attach them to the bulletin board display. Copy the tree pattern on dark green paper and arrange on the board as well.

Generating Ideas: Idea Center

Background for the Teacher

Materials needed: posters, pictures, maps, picture books, magazines, calendars, postcards, children's dictionary, encyclopedia, travel posters and brochures, posters of poems, music, children's poetry books, and any other visual and written material that will stimulate ideas and imaginations

Lesson Presentation

Introduce the idea center to the students. Demonstrate ways to find ideas by exploring in the idea center. Role play with a monologue, such as the following:

I want to create a funny poem, but I need an idea. I will go into the idea center and look around. Hmm . . . I could create a funny poem about the ocean, or maybe about the month of July. Maybe I could create a funny poem about bugs. Here are some funny poems. Oh, here is a funny picture of a dog. The dog looks like he is tired of being pulled around in a wagon. I think I'll create a funny poem about what that dog might be thinking!

Encourage students to visit the idea center often throughout the unit.

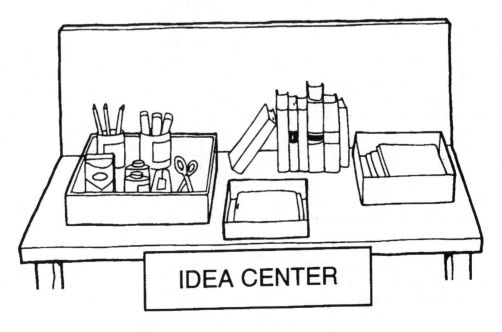

IDEA CENTER

Skill Building: Rhythm and Motion

Background for the Teacher

Rhythm is an important and natural component in poetry. Students will learn to appreciate poetic rhythm by exploring rhythm in motion.

Definition: Rhythm is a regular pattern of stressed and unstressed beats within an imposed structure (a measure of music, a line of poetry).

Materials needed: March! (page 13), Weekday Chant (page 14), books with rhythmic stories (for example, *Clap Your Hands* by Lorinda Bryan Cauley, Putnam Publishing Group, 1992; *Bearobics* by Victoria Parker & Emily Bolan, Putnam, 1999; and *Saturday Night at the Dinosaur Stomp* by Carol Diggory Shields, Candlewick Press, 1997), rhythmic music tapes or CDs, preferably in 4/4 time

Preparation: Reproduce one copy of each worksheet for each student. Gather the materials needed for the lesson.

Lesson Plan

1. Gather students together and tell them to listen carefully as you clap a pattern.

2. Initiate discussion about what you just did. Introduce words like *beat, rhythm,* and *pattern.*

3. Clap a simple beat pattern and ask the students to copy it. Do this several times. Have students take turns clapping a pattern for their classmates to copy. Encourage complex patterns as students become more capable.

4. Practice with more rhythmic activities. Play some rhythmic music and tell the students to clap to the beat. Read a rhythmic story or poem and have them clap to the beat again. Have the students stand and march to the beat of some rhythmic music. You may also play music and allow them to move as they listen.

5. Have the students learn the marches and nursery rhymes on March! As a class, students can march while they chant the lines.

6. Introduce the Weekday Chant to students and have them practice until they can chant and perform the actions in rhythm.

March!

March, march, march, march, march!

I left my wife and forty-two kids alone in the house with no gingerbread!

Left, left, left, right, left!

Pease porridge hot!

Pease porridge cold!

Pease porridge in the pot

Nine days old.

Some like it hot,

Some like it cold,

Some like it in the pot

Nine days old!

Diddle, diddle, dumpling, my son John,

Went to bed with his trousers on!

One shoe off, and one shoe on,

Diddle, diddle, dumpling, my son John.

Weekday Chant

Mon-day, Mon-day, march for fun day
(pat, pat, clap, clap, pat, pat, clap, clap)

1, 2, 3, 4
(march in place four times)

Tues-day, Tues-day, clap by 2's day
(pat, pat, clap, clap, pat, pat, clap, clap)

2, 4, 6, 8
(clap and count by 2's to 8)

Wednes-day, Wednes-day, make a friend day
(pat, pat, clap, clap, pat, pat, clap, clap)

Hello, hola, ciao, aloha
(wave, bow, salute, "hang loose" symbol)

Thurs-day, Thurs-day, jump and turn day
(pat, pat, clap, clap, pat, pat, clap, clap)

North, east, south, west
(jump and face each direction as it is recited)

Fri-day, Fri-day, hop by 5's day
(pat, pat, clap, clap, pat, pat, clap, clap)

5, 10, 15, 20
(hop and count by 5's out loud)

Satur-day, Satur-day, pat your head day
(pat, pat, clap, clap, pat, pat, clap, clap)

1, 2, 3, 4
(pat head four times as you recite the numbers)

Sun-day, Sun-day, number one day
(pat, pat, clap, clap, pat, pat, clap, clap)

10, 20, 30, 40, 50, 60 70, 80, 90, 100!
(clap on each number as you count by tens to 100)

Skill Building: Using Rhyme

Background for the Teacher

Materials needed: Words That Rhyme (pages 16–17), books of children's poetry

Preparation: Reproduce one copy of Words That Rhyme for each student. (Note: The first page of the Words That Rhyme activity is easier than the second one. You may wish to give only the first page, only the second page, or both pages to your students depending on their abilities.) Find examples of rhyming poetry to share orally with your students.

Lesson Plan

1. Begin by reading some children's poetry to your students. Poems by Robert Louis Stevenson or Dr. Seuss are good choices.

2. Ask students to listen for words that rhyme, or that have the same ending sound, as you read them your selection.

3. When you are finished reading, write a list of rhyming words on the board that students have identified.

4. Read each identified word one at a time and have students brainstorm words to rhyme with each word listed, writing the students' suggestions on the board. You may need to begin with an example or two for younger students.

5. Distribute Words That Rhyme to the students. Students may work independently or may need to have their work dictated, depending on their abilities. Tell students that although there is a word bank, there is no right answer for completing the poems.

6. When students have completed their rhymes, ask them to read the rhymes aloud to their classmates.

Words That Rhyme

Can you finish these poems?

I sat on my hat
And now it's _____.

It's snowing on my head!
And now it's time for _____.

I just saw a bug
Crawl under that _____.

I will keep my eye
Upon that piece of _____.

One for the money,
And two for the show,
Three to make ready,
And four to _____.

Jack be nimble,
Jack be _____.
Jack jump over
The _____.

Word Bank

If you have trouble thinking of a word to use,
you may find one here.

• quick	• mat	• rug
• fat	• sled	• bed
• fly	• splat	• flat
• rye	• tie	• Fred
• candlestick	• go	• know
• mow	• pie	• sick

Words That Rhyme *(cont.)*

Complete these poems.

I like to write, I like to _____,
I'm getting better all the _____.

I have a dog, his name is _____.
If I say, "Speak!" he gives a _____!
I took him to the vet last _____,
I picked him up; he was so _____.

I love to play with my pet _____,
Her nose is always twitchy.
We play outside while it is _____,
The grass is very itchy.

Rain

The rain is raining all around,
It falls on field and _____,
It rains on the umbrellas here,
And on the ships at _____.

Robert Louis Stevenson

Word Bank

Use this list to help you complete your rhymes.

rhyme	merry	Flip
sunny	bunny	money
bee	week	slime
scary	night	light
bark	funny	meek
sea	Skip	yip
honey	hairy	pip
tree	time	Clark

#2984 Poetry Writing—Grades 1–2

Skill Building: Hinky Pinky Riddles

Background for the Teacher

Definition: A hinky pinky rhyme is a pair of rhyming words that answer a riddle.

Skills needed: ability to count syllables and rhyme

Materials needed: Student Samples of Hinky Pinky Riddles (page 19), What Do You Call a . . .? (page 20), Response and Assessment (page 22), 3" x 5" (8 cm x 13 cm) cards, sheets of art paper, stapler, markers, crayons

Preparation: Reproduce one copy of each worksheet for each student. Gather together the materials needed for the lesson.

Lesson Plan

1. Write the following riddle on the board, "What is a happy boy?" Let students try to guess the answer. (The answer is "Glad lad.") Have students repeat the answer, noticing the rhyming words. Then tell students that they have created their first hinky pinky rhyme.

2. Brainstorm a list of hinky pinky answers (or use the ones below) and, as a class or in small groups, create questions for them. Then create hinky pinky flashcards with the riddle on one side of a 3" x 5" card and the answer on the other. Have students illustrate the answer sides. Go through the flashcards as a fun, whole class rhyming activity. Place the flashcards in a writing center.

3. Have each student write several hinky pinky rhymes or riddles, with the number depending on ability. Ask students to write their hinky pinky rhymes or riddles on art paper and to illustrate them. Collect these into a class book.

Hinky Pinky Answers

witty kitty	mad dad
lazy daisy	pooch smooch
bug hug	funny bunny
gory story	fright night
sad lad	big pig

Student Samples of Hinky Pinky Riddles

- What do you call a really tiny insect that likes dogs and cats?
  (wee flea)

- What do you call a glass of pink lemonade?
  (pink drink)

- What do you call a smart cat?
  (witty kitty)

- What do you call a cat that eats too much?
  (fat cat)

- What do you call it when someone just keeps singing and singing?
  (long song)

- What do you call candy?
  (sweet treat)

- What do you call someone who steals from the library?
  (book crook)

- What do you say at sunset?
  (sun done)

- What do you call the child who is playing hide-and-go-seek?
  (hid kid)

- What do you call the insect hiding behind the curtain?
  (shy fly)

- When you're just a little bit hungry, what do you want?
  (light bite)

What Do You Call a . . .?

Can you figure out these hinky pinky riddles? (The answers are upside down at the bottom of this page). While you are figuring these out, you may think of some of your own. If you do, write them in the empty square.

1. What do you call Bill when he's sick?

2. What do you call a rabbit that tells jokes?

3. What do you call a purple gorilla?

4. What do you call a large hole?

5. What do you call a squished hat?

Answers: 1. ill Bill 2. funny bunny 3. grape ape 4. big dig 5. flat hat

Content Connections for Hinky Pinky Riddles

Language Arts

Look over your spelling or vocabulary words. Do any of them rhyme? If so, use the pairs as answers to hinky pinky riddles. If not, see if you can create a rhyme for any of your words and then try writing a hinky pinky riddle.

Social Studies

Put the name of a president at the top of your list and then recall as many describing words as you can that fit that president. Next, see if you can think of any rhyming words to match up with the words on your list. For instance, you may think of the word "brave" when you think of Abraham Lincoln. A word that rhymes with "brave" is "slave." Create a hinky pinky riddle for the rhyme, such as "Who did Abraham Lincoln free?" Answer: a brave slave.

Response and Assessment: Hinky Pinky Riddles

Author's Name _____

Poem Title _____

Responder's Name _____ Date _____

Responder:

Did the author . . .

❏ write a question as the first part of the hinky pinky riddle?

❏ write an answer that rhymes?

Author:

Did you . . .

❏ think of a rhyming riddle?

❏ make any changes (revisions) to make your riddle better?

Here is what I think of hinky pinky riddles (check the boxes that say what you think):

❏ I think they are fun.

❏ I think they are hard to create.

❏ I would like to write more hinky pinkies.

Teacher:

_____ The student grasped the idea.

_____ The format is correct.

_____ The student met the standards.

_____ _____

Score _____

Skill Building: Using Rhythm and Meter

Background for the Teacher

Definition: Rhythm is the beat and meter is the pattern of stressed and unstressed (or accented and unaccented) syllables in poetry.

Materials needed: Rhyme Time (pages 24–25), rhythm instruments such as rhythm sticks, tambourines, drums, and spoons, books of children's poetry and nursery rhymes

Preparation: Gather the materials needed for this lesson.

Lesson Plan

1. Clap your hands in a distinctive pattern. Ask the students to listen closely as you do it again, then to echo the pattern in response. Repeat the exercise several times with many different patterns. Invite several students to clap a pattern of their own creation to be copied by the rest of the class.

2. Play music with a strong beat for the students and just have them listen. Allow younger students to stand up and move to the music.

3. Pass out rhythm instruments and have the students experiment with them while listening to the same music.

4. Distribute Rhythm Time to the students. Read each poem aloud, emphasizing the rhythm. Have the students clap the rhythm, and then copy it with their instruments.

5. Put the instruments away and tell students that they will be using their voices as instruments. Read the poem this time by substituting a nonsense sound like *da* or *la* for each syllable. Have the students try it for themselves, reading aloud to them lines from poems (nursery rhymes are good) and having the students repeat the rhythm using the nonsense syllable.

Rhyme Time

Simple Simon

Simple Simon met a pie man,
Going to the fair;
Says Simple Simon to the pie man,
"Let me taste your ware."
Says the pie man to Simple Simon,
"Show me first your penny;"
Says Simple Simon to the pie man,
"Indeed I have not any."
Simple Simon went a-fishing,
For to catch a whale;
All the water he had got
Was in his mother's pail.
He went for water in a sieve
But soon it all fell through;
And now poor Simple Simon
Bids you all adieu.

More practice:

Little Miss Muffet

Little Miss Muffet
Sat on a tuffet,
Eating her curds and whey;
Along came a spider,
Who sat down beside her
And frightened Miss Muffet away.

Rhyme Time *(cont.)*

More practice:

A Farmer Went Trotting

A farmer went trotting upon his grey mare,

Bumpety, bumpety, bump!

With his daughter behind him so rosy and fair,

Lumpety, lumpety, lump!

A raven cried, "Croak!" and they all tumbled down,

Bumpety, bumpety, bump!

The mare broke her knees and the farmer his crown,

Lumpety, lumpety, lump!

Ride a Cock-Horse

Ride a cock-horse to Banbury Cross,

To see a fine lady upon a white horse;

Rings on her fingers and bells on her toes,

And she shall have music wherever she goes.

Wee Willie Winkie

Wee Willie Winkie

Runs through the town,

Upstairs and downstairs,

In his nightgown,

Rapping at the window,

Crying through the lock,

"Are the children in their beds,

For now it's eight o'clock?"

Skill Building: Writing Couplets

Background for the Teacher

Definition: A couplet is two lines of poetry that rhyme.

Skills needed: an understanding of rhyme and rhyming sounds

Materials needed: The Couplet (page 28), Rhyming Couplets (page 29), Student Samples of Couplets (page 30, optional), Storytelling with Couplets (pages 31–33), Response and Assessment (page 36), crayons and markers, scissors, an envelope for each student

Preparation: Reproduce one copy of each worksheet for each student in the class. Gather together the other materials needed. Arrange to take dictation from pre-readers.

Lesson Plan

Prewriting

1. Write a list of rhyming 1- and 2-syllable words on the board or chart paper (see the list on page 27). Have the students come up with many additional rhyming words to match the listed words. Accept nonsense syllables.

2. Read aloud to students several books with strong rhyming patterns (e.g., Dr. Seuss). Discuss any forced rhymes or nonsense words that are used. Discuss the fact that stories can be told in rhyme.

3. Have the students complete The Couplet. Capable readers can work independently, while pre-readers can work in small groups.

Drafting

1. Distribute copies of Rhyming Couplets. Have the students cut the rectangles apart and place them into envelopes labeled with their names.

2. Instruct students to reach into their envelopes and pull out one of the pieces.

3. Have the students write a couplet using their chosen rhyming pair. Assist younger students in creating lines that end with their chosen words.

4. Distribute Storytelling with Couplets. Meet with students individually or in small groups to help them through each step. Allow students to illustrate their stories.

Skill Building: Writing Couplets *(cont.)*

Revising/Editing

1. Have the students read their couplets aloud in class or in small groups. Reading the couplets aloud will help the students hear the rhythm and rhyme.

2. Encourage students to make any desired changes and let them know that in doing this they are revising and editing their work.

Publishing

1. Bind illustrated couplets together into a class poetry book.

2. Encourage students to write and illustrate more couplets, using their rhyming couplets squares or any other rhyming pairs they may think of.

3. Make a bulletin board display of the couplet stories and invite parents and other classes to come and see them.

Simple Rhyming Words

fall	cat	wow	wig
wall	hat	cow	pig
bug	top	toe	float
rug	stop	bow	note
sail	funny	kind	heard
whale	bunny	find	bird
sun	lazy	car	fill
run	daisy	jar	still
flip	in	ball	moon
hip	pin	wall	soon

The Couplet

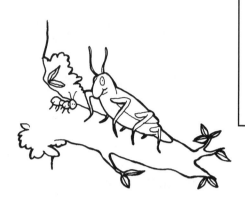

Couplets are lines that always **rhyme**.
With rhyming words to end each **line**.

So write a line, the rules don't **bend**.
With that same rhyme the line must **end**.

Finish the couplets below.

A poem, a poem, I cannot write

I tried and tried all through the _____.

Through the door I tossed the ball

And watched it rolling down the _____.

Up in the tree, I saw my cat

_____.

Grasshoppers, spiders and tiny ants

_____.

Now write your own couplet on the lines below.

_____.

_____.

Rhyming Couplets

Directions: Make copies of this page and cut out the rectangles. Place the rectangles in a folder or envelope in the center. Have the students, individually or in pairs, write two-line rhyming poems using the two words on their rectangle(s).

nice rice	think wink	time climb	asleep deep
bed dread	tight night	toast most	bugs slugs
said ahead	door explore	inside fried	there beware
store ignore	pause jaws	far jar	unload explode
bees knees	page age	easy queasy	bed bread
chair air	fly try	space case	tame game

Student Samples of Couplets

I was swimming down so deep—
It was a dream, I was asleep!

My favorite food in all the world is warm and yummy bread!
I eat it in the morning, then I hide some in my bed!

I love to jump, and play, and yell, and hop upon my pop,
I do it while I can because he'll soon tell me to stop!

Please tell the bugs to go away,
It's time for me to go and play!

I am hungry; my tummy's grumbly;
I can hear it's noisy and rumbly!

I can tell it's time to eat,
How about something sweet?

Storytelling with Couplets

You will be writing a story using rhyming couplets. To begin, think of one of the following:

- something funny or interesting that happened to you recently
- something funny or interesting that happened to someone you know
- a funny or interesting story about a pretend (fictional) character

What is the funny or interesting thing that happened? _____

_____

What happens first in the story? _____

What happens next? _____

How does it end? _____

Write the first two lines of your story here (be brief, and don't worry about rhyming yet):

_____

_____

Write the second two lines of your story here:

_____

_____

If you need more lines, write the next two to four lines of your story here:

_____

_____

_____

_____

Read pages 32–33 to find out how one student, Angie, turned her storytelling lines into rhyming couplets.

Storytelling with Couplets *(cont.)*

Look at what you wrote (page 31) for the first two lines of your poem. Can you think of rhyming words for any of the words in your poem? Here is what one student, Angie, wrote for her first two storytelling lines:

We were eating ice cream cones and my dad wanted to take a picture.

He told my sister and me to stand on the chairs behind my grandma and grandpa.

Here are some rhyming words for the words in her poem:

Cones: *bones, moans, phones, tones*

Ice cream: *sunbeam, seam, gleam, stream, team*

Dad: *bad, glad, mad, lad, pad, sad*

Stand: *band, hand, land, sand*

Chairs: *cares, dares, pairs, stares, stairs, wares*

Here is what Angie wrote for her first two rhyming couplets:

We were licking at our cones, and then we heard our dad

"Stand up upon those chairs!" We thought that he'd gone mad!

On the lines below, write words that rhyme with words in your first two story lines.

_____

_____

Now write a storytelling couplet for the first two lines of your poem, using two of the rhyming words from your list.

_____

_____

Storytelling with Couplets *(cont.)*

To finish telling your story with couplets, you can continue thinking of rhyming words for each part of your story. For example, here is the rest of Angie's story:

> *So, my sister and I stood up on the chairs and we were grinning for the camera. It was a hot day, though, and our dad was taking a long time to take the picture. Suddenly our ice cream scoops fell off our cones and they landed on top of our grandma and grandpa's heads!*

Angie then thought of rhyming words for the rest of her story. Here is her completed poem:

> *We were licking at our cones, and then we heard our dad*
>
> *"Stand up upon those chairs!" We thought that he'd gone mad!*
>
> *We stood up on the chairs and licked our ice cream cones,*
>
> *We watched and then we waited; you should have heard our moans.*
>
> *He took a long, long time, his camera in his hand,*
>
> *Above our grandma and our grandpa we did wait and stand,*
>
> *When suddenly we heard a plop and then our dad said, "Oh!"*
>
> *Our ice cream fell and plopped upon the heads that were below!*

Write more words that rhyme with words in your story below. Use a separate piece of paper if you need more space.

_____

_____

Use the back of this paper to write a draft of your story in couplet form. Be sure to share your poem with a peer before writing a final draft on a clean sheet of paper.

Content Connections for Couplets

Science

Think of something you have learned in science and tell about it using one or more rhyming couplets. You may write about facts, steps of an experiment, or anything about science. Illustrate your poem.

Fine Arts

Look at some examples of fine art. Do any of them inspire a couplet or two? Or maybe you can think of an entire couplet story to write based on a painting. Illustrate your couplet with your own drawing or painting.

Content Connections for Couplets *(cont.)*

Language Arts

Look at a story or journal entry you have written. Write the same story in couplet form. For an extra challenge, trade stories with a classmate, and while he or she writes your story in couplet form, you will do the same with his or her story. Be sure to illustrate your couplet stories.

Social Studies

Choose an event in history that you have been studying and write about it in couplet form. (Take a look at "Paul Revere's Ride" by Henry Wadsworth Longfellow for an example.) If you wish, you may illustrate your poem.

Response and Assessment: Couplets

Author's Name _____

Poem Title_____

Responder's Name _____ Date _____

Responder:

Does the author . . .

❑ use rhyming words at the end of the lines?

❑ use pairs (couplets) of rhyming lines?

Is any part confusing? Why?_____

Could the illustrations be improved? _____

Author:

Have you . . .

❑ read your poem to see if it sounds right?

Does your poem say what you want to say? _____

Did you change anything? What did you change and why?

_____

Complete the following:

The couplet poem was hard to write because: _____

_____

My favorite part of writing a couplet poem was: _____

_____

I would like to write another couplet poem.   **Yes**   **No**

Teacher:

_____ The student uses similar sounds and/or rhymes at the end of the couplet lines.

_____ The student was creative and/or funny.

_____ The student thought of ways to make his or her couplet poem better.

_____ _____

Score _____

Skill Building: Alphabet Poem

Background for the Teacher

Definition: An alphabet poem uses each letter from either the entire alphabet from A to Z, or a portion thereof, to begin a line of poetry on a chosen topic.

Skills needed: an understanding of alphabetical order

Materials needed: Alphabet Squares (page 40), Alphabet Poem Brainstorming worksheet (page 41), Alphabet Poem Draft worksheet (page 42), Response and Assessment (page 45), and old magazines and newspapers

Preparation: Reproduce one copy of each worksheet for each student. Cut out the alphabet squares. Gather together all of the remaining materials.

Lesson Plan

Prewriting

1. Introduce alphabet poems by having students create an alphabetized list about a favorite topic. You may use the Alphabet Poem Brainstorming worksheet or create a list on the board with the entire class. Choose a topic such as "All About Me" for individual students or "Our School" for the whole class.

2. Distribute one letter square from Alphabet Squares to each student. (Start the alphabet over again if you have more than 26 students, or have students work in pairs.)

3. Tell the students to think of a word that starts with their letters, one that relates to the chosen topic. They may write the word on the back of their alphabet squares or dictate them to someone.

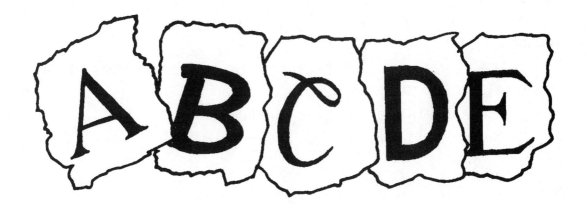

Skill Building: Alphabet Poem *(cont.)*

Drafting

1. On the board or chart paper, write the class alphabet poem by calling each letter of the alphabet in order. The students, or pairs, can call out their words, or they may come up to write them on the board or chart on the appropriate line.

2. When all the assigned letters have been called and the words added to the poem, read the poem aloud. Congratulate the students for having written a poem together. If the poem was written on chart paper, you may wish to have students create illustrations to be glued around the border of the poem.

3. Generate a discussion among the students about how they created the poem. What did they do first? What did they do next? How did they think of words to fit? What did they do last?

4. Distribute the Alphabet Poem Brainstorming worksheet to the students. Tell them to select a topic and to brainstorm words that relate to it.

5. When students are ready, distribute the Alphabet Poem Draft worksheet. Have the students write their own alphabet poems on the worksheet. Younger students will need to dictate their poems.

Revising/Editing

1. The students should share their alphabet poems with responders from class (this may be done orally in small groups for pre-readers). The responders' feedback can be recorded on the Response and Assessment sheet.

2. Encourage students to make any changes they wish, after receiving feedback and before writing a final draft.

Publishing

1. Post the class-generated alphabet poem, along with the illustrations, in a place where all the students can see it.

2. Students may wish to use letters cut from magazines and newspapers to illustrate their individual, or partner alphabet poems. Copies of these poems would make a good classroom book for a writing center.

Student Sample of an Alphabet Poem

Traveling

Airplanes
Bicycles
Cameras
Departures
Elephants
Food
Gardens
Hotels
Islands
Jungles
Kangaroos
Lines
Markets
Natives
Outdoors
Passports
Queues
Rain
Shoes
Tickets
Umbrellas
Views
Windows
X-rays
Yellowstone
Zoos

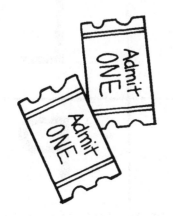

Alphabet Squares

Reproduce this sheet and cut the squares apart to distribute to students. (Note: You will need a second copy if you have more than 26 students, or you can put students in pairs instead.)

A	B	C	D
E	F	G	H
I	J	K	L
M	N	O	P
Q	R	S	T
U	V	W	X
	Y	Z	

Alphabet Poem Brainstorming

The topic you choose will be the title of your alphabet poem. Brainstorm words that relate to your topic. You may use a dictionary, if you wish. Find words that begin with each letter of the alphabet.

_____
Topic

A _____   J _____   S _____

_____   _____   _____

B _____   K _____   T _____

_____   _____   _____

C _____   L _____   U _____

_____   _____   _____

D _____   M _____   V _____

_____   _____   _____

E _____   N _____   W _____

_____   _____   _____

F _____   O _____   X _____

_____   _____   _____

G _____   P _____   Y _____

_____   _____   _____

H _____   Q _____   Z _____

_____   _____   _____

I _____   R _____

_____   _____

Alphabet Poem Draft

Write your alphabet poem on the lines.

Topic _____

_____ _____

_____ _____

_____ _____

_____ _____

_____ _____

_____ _____

_____ _____

Content Connections for Alphabet Poems

Language Arts

Make a list of your classmates in alphabetical order. After each student's name, write a positive word to describe him or her that begins with that letter of the alphabet. For example: Steven-Smart, Kyra-Kind.

Math

Assign each letter of the alphabet a number in order. Create some math equations using letters instead of numbers, for example: A + A = B (1 + 1 = 2).

Content Connections for Alphabet Poems *(cont.)*

Social Studies

Choose a topic from the social studies unit you are studying. See for how many letters of the alphabet you can find a related word. Put the words in alphabetical order and you will have a social studies alphabet poem.

Fine Arts

Listen to lots of different music and make a list of all the different ways you might move to it, such as sway, hop, wiggle, etc. When you have enough words, arrange them in alphabetical order to write a musical movement alphabet poem.

Response and Assessment: Alphabet Poems

Author's Name _____

Poem Title _____

Responder's Name _____ Date _____

Responder:

Did the author . . .

❏ write the poem in alphabetical order?

❏ use one line for each letter of the alphabet?

❏ use creativity and imagination?

Did you enjoy reading this poem? Why? _____

_____

Do you have any suggestions for the author? _____

Author:

Did you make any changes in your poem? _____

Did you enjoy writing this poem? Why or why not? _____

_____

What do you like best about your poem? _____

_____

What was the hardest part of writing this poem? _____

_____

Would you like to write another alphabet poem?   **Yes**   **No**

Teacher:

_____ The student understands the concept of an alphabet
poem.

_____ The student is creative and original.

_____ The student understands the revision process, and has
used it.

_____ _____

Score _____

Skill Building: Personal Poetry

Background for the Teacher

Definition: Personal poetry is any poetry that the author writes about his or her own personal feelings and thoughts on a subject, usually in free verse. For this lesson, however, students will use a structure.

Skills needed: ability to read and write, or the ability to convey personal feelings in dictation

Materials needed: A Poem about Me (page 48); If I Were in Charge of the World (page 49); Personal Poem (page 50); markers; drawing paper; crayons; books of children's poetry such as those by Robert Louis Stevenson, A. A. Milne, and Shel Silverstein

Preparation: Reproduce one copy of each worksheet for each student. Gather art materials and literature needed for the lesson.

Lesson Plan

Prewriting

1. Select several poems for children that are of a personal nature, for example, "Bed in Summer" by Robert Louis Stevenson:

Bed in Summer

In winter I get up at night
And dress by yellow candlelight.

In summer, quite the other way,
I have to go to bed by day.

I have to go to bed and see
The birds still hopping on the tree,

Or hear the grown-up people's feet
Still going past me in the street.

And does it not seem hard to you,
When all the sky is clear and blue,

And I should like so much to play,
To have to go to bed by day?

Skill Building: Personal Poetry *(cont.)*

2. Discuss the poem with the students. Who is speaking in the poem? (The narrator is a child). What do you learn about the narrator from reading the poem? (The narrator is sad that he or she has to go to bed while it is still light outside.)

3. Discuss other examples of personal poetry. If possible, try to locate personal poetry written by older students at your school.

Drafting

1. Distribute copies of A Poem About Me to students. Allow time to discuss the assignment and to begin brainstorming. Take dictation from younger students; older students can work independently.

2. Distribute copies of If I Were in Charge of the World. Discuss, brainstorm, and assign writing the poem as in #1, above.

3. Distribute copies of Personal Poem to students as a challenge.

4. As an additional challenge, assign students to create a form for their own personal poems and then complete them.

Revising/Editing

1. Have students meet in small groups to share their favorite of the three personal poems. Instruct students in ways to offer constructive criticism.

2. Instruct students to make any changes they want after meeting in the writers' groups.

Publishing

1. Instruct students to choose their favorite personal poem and illustrate it. Bind the poems together in a class poetry collection, or post them on a bulletin board display.

2. Publish the poems on a student poetry site on the Internet.

Our Class Collection of Personal Poetry

A Poem About Me

The mixed-up chameleon wanted to be many things it was not. But being what it was not did not make it happy. It found out that being itself was best. Find out about yourself by completing the poem below.

I am _____

_____

and _____

But I am not _____

I like _____

_____

and _____

But I do not like_____

I am happy when _____

_____

and _____

But I am not happy when _____

_____

and _____

I feel good about myself when _____

_____

and _____

If I could be anything, I would be _____

_____

and _____

But, even though I could be anything, I would not be _____

_____

If I Were in Charge of the World

If I were in charge of the world,

I'd cancel _____

_____,

_____ and also

_____.

If I were in charge of the world,

There'd be _____

_____,

_____,

_____ and

_____.

If I were in charge of the world,

You wouldn't have _____.

You wouldn't have _____.

You wouldn't have _____.

Or _____.

You wouldn't even have _____.

If I were in charge of the world,

_____

_____.

And a person who sometimes forgot _____,

And sometimes forgot _____,

Would still be allowed to be

in charge of the world.

Personal Poem

This is a project your family is sure to enjoy. To create it, you will need the following:

- a sheet of medium-weight drawing paper, about 14" x 11" (36 cm x 28 cm)
- a photograph of yourself that measures about 4" x 6" (10 cm x 15 cm)
- pencils, pens, markers, or crayons
- the Personal Poem form (page 51)

What is a personal poem? Read the example below.

Jason
Affectionate, shy, athletic
Sibling of
Michael, Chris, Kiera
Lover of
Soft, warm, furry pets, rainy days,
Cool pools
Who feels
Love, affection, kindness
Who needs
Affection, understanding, generosity
Who gives
Love, friendship, affection
Who fears
large waves, darkness, unknown things
Who would like to see
The tops of clouds, the ground from above
The blackness of space.
Buffington

After writing your poem on a practice paper, glue your photograph to the drawing paper and write your poem beside it. Use fancy letters for your first and last names. Use markers or crayons to add art in the leftover spaces on the paper.

Personal Poem *(cont.)*

To begin, fill in the following blanks:

First name

_____

List three adjectives about yourself

_____, _____, _____,

Sibling (or child/grandchild) of

_____

Lover of

_____

Who feels

_____

Who needs

_____

Who gives

_____

Who fears

_____

Who would like to see

_____

Last name

_____

(The examples on page 52 will give you more ideas.)

Student Samples of Personal Poetry

A Poem About Me

I am Austin,
And I am a boy who likes to play.
But I am not a boy who likes to be quiet.
I like applesauce
And chocolate milk.
But I do not like going to the doctor.
I am happy when my mom wrestles with me
And when we go to the park.
But I am not happy when I have to get a shot
And when I have to eat my vegetables.
I feel good about myself when I take a nap
And when I eat dinner.
If I could be anything, I would be a fire engine driver
And a daddy.
But, even though I could be anything, I would not be a robber.

If I Were in Charge of the World

If I were in charge of the world, I'd cancel school and also kickball.
If I were in charge of the world, there'd be more books and more chocolate and more swingsets.
If I were in charge of the world,
You wouldn't have liver.
You wouldn't have little brothers.
You wouldn't have ants
Or flies.
You wouldn't even have storms.
If I were in charge of the world,
We would get to eat pizza all the time.
And a person who sometimes forgot her math homework
And sometimes forgot to clean her room
Would still be allowed to be
In charge of the world.

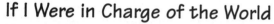

Content Connections for Personal Poems

Language Arts

You can write an autobiography (a report about your life) by writing a personal poem that tells all about you. Try it and be sure to include things like your hair and eye color; your birthday; your parents' names; the names of your brothers and sisters; your grandparents' names; where you are from; your favorite colors, foods, activities, hobbies, school subjects, etc. You can also write a biography poem about someone you know.

Math

Write a personal poem by using a personal number to start each line. The personal numbers can be such things as the following: the month you were born, your favorite number, the number of people who live with you, the number of pets you have, etc. After the number on each line, write what the number means. For example: 8, the month of my birthday; 4, the number of cats in our house; etc. When you finish your poem, add up all the numbers and make that your title.

Content Connections for
Personal Poems *(cont.)*

Social Studies

Choose someone from history that you have studied recently. Find out some things about this person and then write a personal poem as if the person wrote it. You may use one of the personal poetry forms (pages 48–50), if you wish.

Science

Write a personal poem about the things you like in science (for example, rocks, insects, mammals, oceans, etc.). Or, choose a favorite science topic and write a personal poem that explains why you like it so much.

Response and Assessment: Personal Poems

Author's Name _____

Poem Title _____

Responder's Name _____ Date _____

Responder:

Did the author . . .

❑ write in a personal way?

❑ help you to better understand the author?

What do you think will make the poem better?_____

_____

What do you like best about the poem? _____

_____

Author:

What changes did you make in your poem? _____

_____

What do you like about your poem? _____

_____

What was the hardest part about writing a personal poem?

_____

Would you like to write another personal poem?   **Yes**   **No**

Teacher:

_____ Student understood and followed the form.

_____ Student included personal expression.

_____ Student wrote additional personal poems in other
          forms.

_____ _____

Score _____

Skill Building: Concrete Poetry

Background for the Teacher

Definition: Concrete poetry is poetry written in a shape that relates to the topic of the poem.

Skills needed: no special skills needed

Materials needed: Student Samples of Concrete Poems (page 58), Creating a Concrete Poem (page 59–60), Response and Assessment (page 62), books of poetry that contain examples of concrete poems, overhead transparencies, rulers, stencils and drafting aids, art paper, colored pencils, markers, chart paper, butcher or poster paper

Preparation: Create overhead transparencies of student samples (page 58). Reproduce a copy of Creating a Concrete Poem for each student. Gather other materials needed for lesson.

Lesson Plan

Pre-writing

1. Introduce students to concrete poetry by sharing the student samples and other examples. Ask the students what they notice about concrete poetry. What makes it different from other forms of poetry?

2. Have students brainstorm a topic for a concrete poem. Then have them brainstorm a form for the poem to take.

3. As a whole class, create a concrete poem on chart paper. Display the example as a reference.

Drafting

1. Distribute copies of Creating a Concrete Poem to students. Have students create a "blueprint" of the poem they will be creating. For younger students, work in small groups or individually to complete the plans.

2. Point out to students that there are stencils to use if they wish to write their poems within an outlined shape. Some students will prefer to write lines that form a design instead.

Skill Building: Concrete Poetry *(cont.)*

Drafting *(cont.)*

3. When the students have written their poems, have them share them in writers' workshops, or with a partner. They should also share the forms that their poems will take.

Revising/Editing

1. Encourage students to make any changes to make their poems better.

Final Draft

1. When the students are ready for the final work, distribute the art paper, markers, colored pencils, stencils, rulers, etc. (Work with small groups of students if they are pre-readers.)

2. Have them write their poems in the shapes or forms that they have chosen.

3. Encourage color and creativity.

Publishing

1. The finished concrete poems will make an unusual and interesting display. Display the poems for an open house and/or invite students in other grades to come and see the exhibit.

Student Samples of Concrete Poems

The
Tree in
My backyard is
Very green and bushy.
The birds hide in its green
Branches and sing their birdie
Songs all day long, and then at night
They make their beds in the lower branches
And the tree covers them with its arms and hums
A lullaby.

The blades of grass are waving to me while the sun lights them up like little green lights. Then I would make a bed on the soft, brown earth and nap in the waving grass. I want to run outside and play in the grass and hide between the blades and roll on the cushion-y green pillows that smell like spring.

Creating a Concrete Poem

I would like to write a concrete poem about:

_____

Here are some ideas I have about how my concrete poem will look:

_____

_____

_____

Here are some sketches that might work for my concrete poem:

_____

Here are some things I would like to say in my concrete poem:

_____

_____

Creating a Concrete Poem *(cont.)*

Here is my concrete poem:

Content Connections for Concrete Poems

Social Studies

Choose a state. It may be one that you have learned about, or your favorite state. Look at a map of your state and draw its outline to fill a piece of art paper. Don't worry about getting the state outline perfect, just draw or trace what you see as the shape. On another piece of paper, write a poem about the state. You may say anything you'd like about the state, such as a memory from a visit; the state's features (mountains, lakes, cities, etc.); or something about the state flower, bird, motto, or products. Now, fit your poem inside the shape of the state.

Math

Write a poem that would use a lot of numbers (like how many cats you have, how many grandparents have visited, your address, etc.). Choose a geometric shape (like a triangle, rectangle, or circle, etc.) and write your poem inside that shape. Write the numbers in a bright color. When you finish, add up all the numbers and use the total as the title of your poem.

Response and Assessment: Concrete Poems

Author's Name _____

Poem Title _____

Responder's Name _____ Date _____

Responder:

Did the author . . .

❏ choose a shape or a pattern that matches the topic?

❏ show imagination?

Did you enjoy reading what the author wrote? _____

Do you have any suggestions for improving the concrete poem?

_____

Author:

What changes did you make to your concrete poem? _____

_____

Did you enjoy creating the poem? _____

What was the hardest part of creating your concrete poem?

_____

What do you like best about your poem?

_____

Would you like to create another concrete poem?

Yes   No

Teacher:

_____ The student understands the concept of concrete poetry.

_____ The student was creative and imaginative.

_____ The student made revisions to improve his or her poem.

_____ _____

Score _____

Skill Building: Five Senses Poem

Background for the Teacher

Definition: In a five senses poem, each line describes the topic as it appeals to one of the senses. Almost any topic can be used for a five senses poem. This lesson will teach students to write a five senses poem about a favorite time of the year.

Skills needed: knowledge of the five senses, brainstorming

Materials needed: Senses Scavenger Hunt (page 65), My Favorite Time of the Year (page 67), Response and Assessment (page 70), colored pencils, markers, crayons, construction paper in various colors, scissors, glue or tape

Preparation: Reproduce a copy of Senses Scavenger Hunt and My Favorite Time of the Year for each student. Gather other materials needed.

Lesson Plan

Pre-writing

1. Initiate a discussion of the five senses with students. You may wish to read a book like *My Five Senses* by Aliki.

2. While students remain in the classroom, list the things they can detect with their senses. Ask them questions like, What do you hear? (cars outside, children in another classroom, a humming computer, etc.). Ask questions for each of the senses and encourage students to pay attention.

3. Choose, in advance, where to hold a five senses scavenger hunt (a playground area, certain sections of the school, within the classroom, etc.). Distribute copies of Senses Scavenger Hunt to individual students or teams. Give the students a time period in which to find as many of the items as possible. They may fill in the blanks with their findings, or report back to adult assistants.

4. Distribute copies of My Favorite Time of the Year to individual students or student pairs, along with crayons, colored pencils, and markers.

Skill Building: Five Senses Poem *(cont.)*

5. Discuss with students the four seasons and holidays. Instruct them to choose a favorite time of the year. Have each student draw a picture of his or her chosen time of the year in the box at the top of the page.

6. Have the students fill in the blanks about what they see, taste, feel, etc. during their favorite times. Take dictation from younger students.

7. Share the sample five senses poems with students. Point out to them that there is one line for each of the five senses.

Drafting

1. Have the students write their five senses poems using the My Favorite Time of the Year worksheets as reference. Take dictation from younger students.

Editing/Revising

1. When the students have written their five senses poems, have them meet with partners or small groups to share and offer feedback.

2. Encourage revisions and meet individually with younger students.

Publishing

1. Create a display of the five senses poems and their illustrations for all the students to see.

2. Create greeting cards using five senses poems appropriate to the time of year or an approaching holiday. The illustration can go on the outside and the poem on the inside of the card.

Senses Scavenger Hunt

Find a sound that is very soft.

_____

Find a smell that is sweet.

_____

Find something that looks bright and light.

_____

_____

Find something that feels rough.

_____

Find something that might taste sweet (but don't taste it!).

_____

Find a sound that repeats itself over and over again.

_____

_____

Find something that looks funny.

_____

Find something that smells flowery.

_____

Find something that feels slippery or smooth.

_____

_____

Find something that might taste yucky (but don't taste it!).

_____

_____

_____

_____

Student Samples of Five Senses Poems

Summertime

I feel the buttery, warm sunshine,

I see the clear, blue sky,

I hear crickets and birds chirping and mosquitoes humming,

I taste juicy watermelons and sour lemonade,

I smell the grass being cut.

Winter

I hear the silence of a new snowy blanket,

I taste hot chocolate,

I smell wet wool,

I hear dripping, cracking icicles,

I feel myself shivering!

Back to School

I smell new shoes and new books,

I taste cafeteria pizza,

I see everyone is bigger now,

I hear the bell ringing.

My Favorite Time of the Year

Directions: Complete and illustrate the lines below, using a favorite time of the year for ideas.

Sight:

_____   _____

_____   _____

Sound:

_____   _____

_____   _____

Taste:

_____   _____

_____   _____

Smell:

_____   _____

_____   _____

Feel:

_____   _____

_____   _____

Content Connections for Five Senses Poems

Language Arts

Choose a favorite book that you have recently enjoyed and write a five senses poem about it. You will have written a book report!

Fine Arts

Your teacher will play some music for you. Close your eyes and listen carefully. Can you think of ways to describe the music using your five senses (or most of them)? What does the music sound like? Does it sound peaceful or is it busy or angry? Does it feel smooth and silky, or bumpy? Would the music appear colorful, or just one or two colors? If you could smell it, would it smell like wool or the sky before a storm, or would it smell like flowers or candy? If you could taste it, would it taste salty, sweet, sour, or bitter?

Content Connections for
Five Senses Poems *(cont.)*

Social Studies

Pick a period of time in history. You may choose a time that you have studied, or your teacher may give you a time period. Brainstorm some ideas about this time period. Write a five senses poem about what it would be like if you were in that period of time in history. What would it look like, smell like, taste like, etc.?

Science

Pretend that you are a scientist and that you are investigating a strange substance or object, for instance, peanut butter. Without naming the subject of your investigation, describe it using the five senses in a five senses poem. Let your classmates try to guess what the object or substance is.

Response and Assessment: Five Senses Poems

Author's Name _____

Poem Title _____

Responder's Name _____ Date _____

Responder:

Did the author . . .

❏ use one line for each of the five senses?

❏ write only about the topic?

Did you enjoy the author's five senses poem? Why? _____

_____

Do you have any ideas about how to make it better? _____

_____

Author:

Did you . . .

❏ make any changes to make your poem better?

❏ use all five senses?

What was the hardest part of writing a five senses poem?

_____

What do you like best about your poem? _____

_____

Would you like to write another five senses poem?

               Yes   **No**

Teacher:

_____ The student used all five senses.

_____ The student was creative and imaginative.

_____ The student stayed on topic.

_____ _____

Score _____

Skill Building: Word-List Poem

Background for the Teacher

Definition: A word-list poem is one in which the topic is determined by words "pinched" at random (see page 73).

Skills needed: ability to find a relationship between words and write or dictate a poem

Materials needed: Word-List Poem (pages 73–75 or pages 73 and 75, depending on ability level of your students), Student Samples of Word-List Poems (page 76), Response and Assessment (page 78), construction paper, glue, writing paper, markers, crayons

Preparation: Reproduce one copy of each worksheet for each student. Gather other materials for the lesson.

Lesson Plan

Pre-writing

1. Write a sample word-list poem with your students. Have students brainstorm several words at random. Then demonstrate how to use those words in a poem, writing it on the board or a piece of chart paper. Use the form of poetry that will be the most appropriate for the ability level of your students.

2. Distribute copies of pages 73–75 or pages 73 and 75 to students. Have students cut apart the word lists. Direct students to take a "pinch" of words according to the directions, or simply have each student randomly take three words.

3. Introduce and demonstrate clustering to the students before they fill in the rest of the page with their own clustering.

Drafting

1. When students have clustered and appear ready to write their poems, distribute paper for their first drafts. You may wish to assign a certain number of lines or stanzas or a form of poetry, based upon your students' abilities.

2. Instruct students to write a first draft and to be sure to use all of their words in their poems.

Skill Building:
Word-List Poem *(cont.)*

Revising/Editing

1. Have the students meet in small writers' groups or with partners to share their word-list poems. Meet with each group to offer guidance for writers' workshops with students who are emergent writers.

2. Have the students fill out the assessment forms.

3. Encourage students to make any revisions they want to make before writing the final drafts.

Publishing

1. Distribute paper for the students' final drafts.

2. You may also distribute paper for an illustration to go with the poem. The students may then mount their poems and illustrations on colored construction paper.

3. Create a bulletin board display of the students' word-list poems.

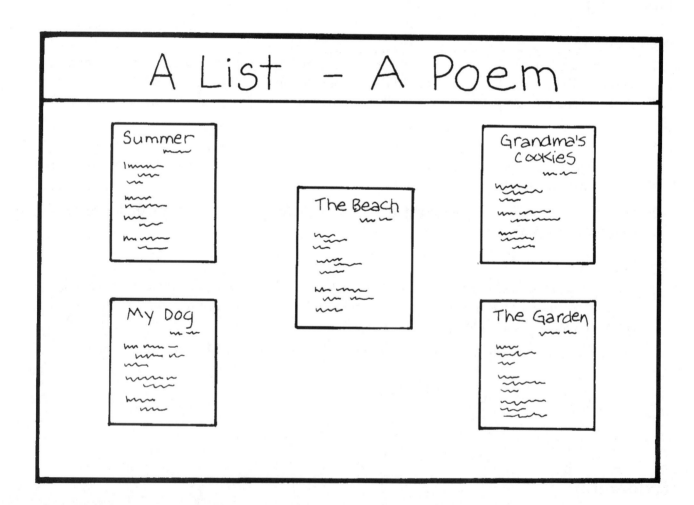

Word-List Poem

Your teacher will give you the opportunity to reach into a basket or box and take a "pinch" of words. Reach in and take a few of the word slips. While other students are "pinching" their words, write your words in the boxes below.

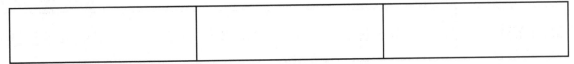

Now that you have written them down, you can allow your teacher to collect the slips. Look at your words. Can you find any relationships among them? It may be difficult, but use your imagination. You can do it.

Now, you can make a word web. Decide which word in your box will be the theme of your web and write it in the center circle of the web. The words you write in the other circles should relate to the theme. Think about how the other words fit with the theme and write them in the outer circles. Fill in the rest of the circles with any other words you wish.

After brainstorming and completing your web, take a piece of paper and, using the words you pinched, write a poem. You can write any kind of poem you like. You don't have to use every word you thought of, but you should use all of the words you "pinched."

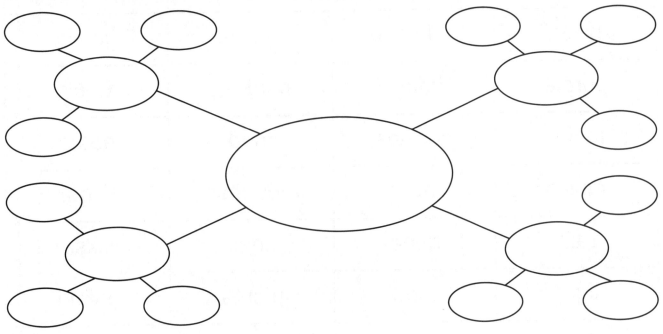

Extension: Illustrate your poem. You can also use "pinched" words to write a creative story. To make it easier, choose only two or three words. To make it more challenging, choose more words.

Word-List Poem (cont.)

Teacher Note: Use this page or page 75 depending on the ability of your students. Make five to ten copies of this page; cut the words on each page apart and place them into their own empty box. Divide your class by the number of boxes. Each group of students will have a complete set of words without duplicates.

baseball	spider	ice cream	impossible
vacation	tornado	grandparents	bird
laugh	monster	bubbles	sing
sneeze	sneakers	peanuts	toy
telephone	giggle	corncob	balloon
pancake	dog	stripes	party
hopscotch	clouds	elephant	skips
pizza	caboose	snow	gorilla
purple	daffodil	rainbow	book
moon	cookies	mud	bottle
music	river	mountain	wagon
rain	huge	shell	quicksand
light	snow	plums	gallop

Word-List Poem (cont.)

Teacher Note: Use this page or page 74 depending on the ability of your students. Make five to ten copies of this page; cut the words on each page apart and place them into their own empty box. Divide your class by the number of boxes. Each group of students will have a complete set of words without duplicates.

ball	mud	sun	foot
rain	bunny	play	zoo
bubbles	smile	sing	movies
grass	hugs	worm	tree
yellow	soft	wind	house
butterflies	noisy	shoes	bells
bath	cuddly	dirty	socks
toes	jump	monster	cookies
colors	book	cat	red
toy	spoon	clouds	taste
apple	game	flowers	kite
dark	sandwich	big	nap
pictures	blue	merry-go-round	song

Student Samples of Word-List Poems

Derek picked the following words for his poem: *puppies, weeds,* and *toes.* Here is Derek's poem.

I went to play outside, the sun called me,
"It's been so long, come outside!"
I took off my shoes and wiggled my toes,
The weeds scraped at my ankles.
It felt so good and happy that I rolled
In the grass like a bunch of puppies!

Samantha picked the words *birds, babies,* and *rain.* Here is her poem.

It was raining so hard that
The birds went to hide.
I couldn't hear their chirping,
But wait, what was that chirping sound?
Babies! Two mothers with strollers
Went pushing by, and happy babies,
Under umbrellas, were chirping like birds!

Landry picked the words *green, peep,* and *window.* Here is his poem.

Outside my window a fat cat sat,
And sang his song of loneliness.
I opened my window and said, "Scat!"
But he only stopped singing.
He looked at me with eyes of green,
As if to say, "I dare you!"
I tried to give him a look so mean,
But still he sat and stared.
Then I cried, "I need some sleep!
And you must go away!"
And so he left without a peep,
Never to be seen again!

Content Connections for Word-List Poems

Social Studies

Choose a topic that you have been learning about in social studies. Make a list of words related to that topic. Cut them apart and put them in a box or hat. Mix them up and "pinch" a few words. Look at your words and think of how you can write a word-list poem about your social studies topic using those words.

Language Arts

Think of someone you'd like to write a poem about. You may want to write a poem about your mother for Mother's Day or your father for Father's Day. Or, maybe you'd like to write a poem about a grandparent, special friend, aunt, or teacher. Begin by making a list of words that are related to that person. They could be words that describe the person; words he or she says; or words that describe things that he or she owns, likes, etc. After you have made a list, cut the words apart and put them in a box or hat. Pinch a few words and write a poem that includes those words. Be sure to decorate your poem and give it as a gift.

Response and Assessment: Word-List Poems

Author's Name _____

Poem Title _____

Responder's Name _____ Date _____

Responder:

Did the author . . .

❏ use all the words that were "pinched"?

❏ stay on topic?

Did you enjoy reading the poem? Why? _____

_____

Do you have any suggestions for improving the poem?_____

Author:

Did you make any changes to make your poem better? _____

_____

Did you enjoy writing your word-list poem? _____

What do you like best about your poem? _____

_____

What was the hardest part about writing your poem? _____

_____

Would you like to write another word-list poem?   **Yes**   **No**

Teacher:

_____ The student was creative and original.

_____ The student revised his or her poem.

_____ The student expressed himself or herself well.

_____

Score _____

Skill Building: Acrostic Poem

Background for the Teacher

Definition: An acrostic poem's title or topic is written in capital letters vertically down the page. Each line then begins with one of the letters in the title or the topic.

Skills needed: No specific skills are needed.

Materials needed: Student Samples of Acrostic Poetry (page 81), Acrostic Poem Work Sheet (page 82), Response and Assessment (page 84), drawing paper, markers, colored pencils, crayons, glue, alphabet stencils, one sheet of lined paper for each student that has his or her name written vertically down the left side of the paper

Preparation: Reproduce one copy of each worksheet for each student. Gather materials needed for the lesson.

Lesson Plan

Prewriting

1. Write a simple word like *cat* on the board. Have the students read the word aloud together.

2. Now, write the word vertically and make sure that students are still able to recognize it.

3. Explain to students that you will be using the word *cat* to write an acrostic poem. Erase the board and write the word *cat* vertically in all capital letters.

4. Encourage students to help you write your poem by having them think of words that describe cats and begin with the letter **C**. When you have chosen a word, write it horizontally across from the letter **C**. Do this for each of the letters to complete the acrostic poem.

5. Demonstrate how to write an acrostic poem about a person. Choose one or two students (star of the week, birthday boy or girl) to come forward. As a class, write an acrostic poem on the board for these students. When they are completed and satisfactory to both of the students, they may copy their acrostic poems on the appropriate lines. (Write the poems for pre-writing students.)

STAR OF THE WEEK

Skill Building: Acrostic Poem *(cont.)*

6. The remaining students may then write acrostic poems about themselves, using their own names, or you may wish to pair the students and have them write about each other.

7. Share the student samples of acrostic poems with students. Discuss the many ways that acrostic poems may be written. Encourage creative ideas.

Drafting

1. Brainstorm with students a list of topics for their acrostic poems. Approaching holidays, sports, or names of significant people will work well. With younger students, choose a simple topic for them and discuss ideas related to that topic in order to generate ideas.

2. Distribute copies of the Acrostic Poem Worksheet to students. With younger students, you may wish to fill in the boxes before making copies, or you may wish to fill in one copy of the worksheet with a sample acrostic poem on the topic. Allow more freedom for older students. Instruct them to write their topic/title in the boxes on the left-hand side of the paper (they don't need to use all of the boxes).

3. Next, the students will fill in the lines to finish their acrostic poems.

4. Distribute art materials and have the students illustrate their poems.

Revising/Editing

1. Before students make final copies of their poems, have them meet in small groups to share them. Encourage positive feedback and suggestions.

2. Allow time for students to make any revisions they may wish to make in their poems.

Publishing

1. Have students illuminate (or create fancy stenciled letters of) the capital letters in their acrostic poems. Display their creations on a bulletin board or bind them into a class book.

Student Samples of Acrostic Poems

Car

Climbing in,
All my family,
Rrrr-rrrrr!

Birds

Bugs for breakfast,
Insects for lunch,
Red feathers and brown,
Dinner is worms,
Singing all the time anyway!

Cassie

Cuddly,
Adorable,
Sweet,
Sassy,
Itchy and,
Eating.

Crayons

Colors everywhere,
Red to make hair,
And
Yellow for eyes,
Orange to make teeth,
Now I've colored my monster,
Scary, huh?

Father

Fixing fried potatoes for breakfast,
Always going to work,
Takes me to a ball game,
Helps me with homework,
Early in the morning he gets up,
Ready to take care of me!

Acrostic Poem Worksheet

Write your title on the first line, and then write the title in the boxes that go down the page.   Write each line of your acrostic poem on the lines next to each box.

_____

☐ _____

☐ _____

☐ _____

☐ _____

☐ _____

Content Connections for Acrostic Poems

Social Studies

Think of a person whom you have read about recently. He or she may be an inventor, explorer, author, or leader. Find some interesting things about the person and write an acrostic poem about him or her. (You may use only the first or last name of the person, if you wish, but write the entire name in the title.)

Science

Choose a topic from nature, such as an insect or flower. Write its name as your title and, after you have found some information about your topic, write an acrostic poem that tells a little about it.

Language Arts

You can make a book report by writing an acrostic poem. Choose a character from a book you've read recently, and brainstorm about the character. What does he or she look like? What does the character like to do and say? What does the character like to eat? What kinds of problems does the character have? Write the character's name in a column along the left side of your paper and then complete the poem, using each letter of the character's name to begin the lines of your poem.

Response and Assessment: Acrostic Poems

Author's Name _____

Poem Title _____

Responder's Name _____ Date _____

Responder:

Did the author . . .

❏ begin each line with the correct letter?

❏ write about the topic?

❏ use his or her imagination?

What suggestions do you have for this poem?_____

_____

Author:

Did you . . .

❏ make any changes before writing your final copy?

❏ use one letter from the topic/title for each line of the poem?

What was the hardest part of writing your poem? _____

_____

Would you like to write another acrostic poem?   **Yes**   **No**

Teacher:

_____ Student has the general idea about acrostic poems.

_____ Student is creative and imaginative.

_____ Student understands the revision process.

_____ _____

Score _____

Skill Building: Counting Sounds

Background for the Teacher

Definition: The sounds found in syllables create the rhythm and meter of poetry.

Materials needed: How Many Syllables? (page 86), Sound Counting Fun (page 87), highlighter markers, colored markers and pencils

Preparation: Reproduce one copy of each worksheet for each student. Gather other materials needed for the lesson.

Lesson Plan

Pre-writing

1. Write the following words on the chalkboard or overhead projector: *dog, puppy, elephant, alligator, hippopotamus.*

2. Read the words aloud, emphasizing the syllables, and write the number of syllables after each word. Ask students if they can guess what you were counting. If students have trouble understanding, offer sound clues. For instance, say the word *puppy*, then use a nonsense syllable to say the syllables, *dah-dah.*

3. Once they grasp the concept, have them say their own words aloud as they try various methods of counting syllables. Count syllables by raising fingers, putting a hand under the chin while saying the word, or clapping.

4. Distribute copies of How Many Syllables? to students. Have students complete the activity as individuals, with partners, or in small groups.

5. When students have finished, go over the activity as a whole class.

Drafting

1. Distribute copies of Sound Counting Fun. This activity closes the gap between counting syllables and writing haiku. If your students are ready to proceed to haiku, you may wish to use this activity as a review.

How Many Syllables?

Count how many syllables are in the words below. Write your answer in the box after each word.

hat ☐   dinner ☐

train ☐   hopscotch ☐

flower ☐   pizza ☐

elephant ☐   baby ☐

skateboard ☐   ice cream cone ☐

drum ☐   spaghetti ☐

library ☐   alligator ☐

Count how many syllables are in each line below. Write your answer in the box after each line.

Twinkle, twinkle, ☐   Hey diddle, diddle, ☐

Little star, ☐   The cat and the fiddle, ☐

How I wonder ☐   The cow jumped over
                           the moon; ☐

What you are! ☐   The little dog laughed ☐

Up above ☐

The world so high, ☐   To see such sport, ☐

Like a diamond ☐   And the dish ran away
                           with the spoon. ☐

In the sky. ☐

Sound Counting Fun

A syllable is a unit of sound that makes a beat when pronounced in a word. You can count syllables with your fingers. Another way to count syllables is to put your hand under your chin as you say the word. Each time your chin moves down, that's one syllable. However you like to count the sounds, write the number of syllables in each of these lines:

Humpty Dumpty _____

Sat on a wall, _____

Humpty Dumpty _____

Had a great fall. _____

Now, write a word or a phrase to match the number of syllables. The first two have been done for you as examples. Be sure to count the sounds to make sure what you wrote matches the number. If it doesn't, try again.

4   I want ice cream! _____

3   gorilla _____

4   _____

2   _____

3   _____

6   _____

5   _____

1   _____

7   _____

5   _____

3   _____

1   _____

4   _____

2   _____

3   _____

5   _____

7   _____

5   _____

Skill Building: Haiku

Background for the Teacher

Definition: Haiku is an unrhymed, three-line poem about a topic in nature. (For younger poets, you may wish to broaden the topic.) The first and third lines are five syllables each. The second line is seven syllables.

Skills needed: ability to count syllables

Materials needed: Create-a-Haiku Kit (page 90), Haiku Frame (page 92), Student Samples of Haiku (page 91), Response and Assessment (page 95), 3" x 5" (8 cm x 13 cm) cards, photos, travel magazines, calendar photos of nature, art paper and materials (felt pens, charcoal, water color, etc.)

Preparation: Reproduce one copy of each worksheet for each student. Collect an assortment of pictures depicting nature and laminate them for durability, if you wish. Gather other materials needed for the lesson.

Lesson Plan

Prewriting

1. Review syllable-counting with students.

2. Write the number 5 on about sixty-five 3" x 5" (8 cm x 13 cm) cards. Write the number 7 on about thirty-five cards. Mix the cards together and have each student draw one card.

3. Brainstorm some nature topics with the class, and write the ideas on the board.

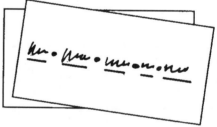

4. The students who drew the number 5 will write a five-syllable phrase about nature. Those who drew the number 7 will write a seven-syllable phrase about nature. Take dictation and provide individual assistance for younger students.

5. Call upon a student with a five-syllable phrase to come forward. Write the student's phrase on the board.

6. Ask the students if anyone has written a seven-syllable phrase that seems like it might go with the phrase on the board. (The phrases may not create strict haiku, but may create unexpectedly interesting poems.)

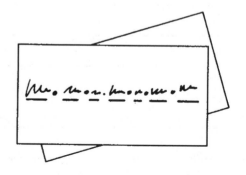

Skill-Building: Haiku *(cont.)*

7. Once a seven-syllable phrase is on the board, ask if students have a five-syllable phrase that will work as the final line of a haiku.

8. You may wish to collect the student-generated haiku poetry and create a poetry book for the class.

9. Distribute copies of Create-a-Haiku Kit and have students work on the activity individually or in pairs. Offer individual help for younger students and take dictation, as needed. You may wish to use only the easier ones for younger students (and create a few more, if you wish).

10. If your students need more practice, go over the activity as a class, brainstorming for words and lines that can fill in the blanks.

Drafting

1. After students have met in writers' workshops, distribute copies of the Haiku Frame. Again, with younger students, take dictation, or have the students copy from one of their drafts.

Revising/ Editing:

1. Have the students meet in small groups or in pairs, to share their work. Encourage helpful commentary.

2. Allow students time to make any revisions they may wish to make.

Publishing

1. Have the students color their haiku frames. You may wish to provide the students with large sheets of art paper to decorate with watercolors, etc., and use as a frame on which to mount the haiku.

2. Create a bulletin board display of the students' poems.

3. Hold a "Haiku Festival" and have the students read their haiku poems to the class and show their illustrations. (For emergent readers, read the haiku for them and allow them to show their art.)

Create-a-Haiku Kit

You are about to create poetry called *haiku*. A haiku is created so that:

The first line has five syllables.

The second line has seven syllables.

And the last line has five syllables.

Strict haiku is written about nature, especially something beautiful, but it can be about other things as well.

Fill in the spaces below with whatever you think will complete the haiku poems. Just remember to have five syllables for the first and last line, and seven syllables for the middle, or second, line every time.

Sitting on a _____,

I saw a spider _____ ing

Its web of beauty.

A bird is _____ ing,

I hear it calling to me,

" _____," it says.

The waves reach up high,

The blue sky smiles on them.

_____

The trees have music,

I hear it when the wind blows,

_____

Student Samples of Haiku

Green leaves are waving,
They are shining in the sun,
They play until dark.

The cat walks to me,
And mews for me to notice,
I pet and she purrs.

The rain is falling,
It beats against the rooftop,
Heaven is crying.

I dig up the soil,
And put tiny seeds inside,
The earth opens wide.

I hear the quiet,
Rushing through the green forest,
And then my soul sings.

The ants are building,
I watch their busy working,
'Til they've built a hill.

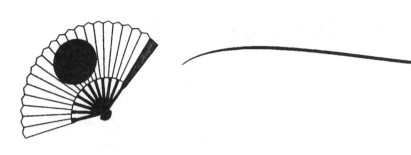

Haiku Frame

_____

_____

_____

Content Connections for Haiku

Science

Choose a topic that you have been studying in science, such as a mountain, weather, a plant or animal, etc. Brainstorm a list of words that would describe your topic. Circle your favorite words and write a haiku about your topic.

Social Studies

Choose a geographical area that you have been studying. It could be a state or country, or it could be a kind of environment, such as the desert, mountains, plains, meadows, etc. After you have chosen your topic, brainstorm a list of words that are related to your topic. Write a haiku about your topic.

Content Connections for Haiku *(cont.)*

Language Arts

Think of the last time you enjoyed being in nature (camping, swimming, or taking a walk) with a friend or family member. Write a haiku that describes what you remember about that. Write it on some paper with a watercolor or illustration you have prepared, and give it as a gift to that friend or family member.

Fine Arts

Look carefully at a beautiful painting. Think about what it reminds you of, how it makes you feel, and what you like about it. Write a haiku poem inspired by the painting. Your poem can describe the painting or how it makes you feel, or your poem can be about something that you thought of when you saw the painting.

Response and Assessment: Haiku

Author's Name _____

Poem Title _____

Responder's Name _____ Date _____

Responder:

Did the author . . .

❑ include 5 syllables in the first line?

❑ include 7 syllables in the second line?

❑ include 5 syllables in the third line?

❑ write about something related to nature?

Do you have any ideas that would make the haiku better?

_____

_____

Author:

Before you wrote your final copy, did you . . .

❑ make any changes to improve your haiku?

Did you enjoy writing your haiku? _____

What was the hardest part about it? _____

_____

Would you like to write another haiku?   **Yes**   **No**

Teacher:

_____ The student followed the proper form.

_____ The student used his or her imagination.

_____ The student was descriptive.

_____ _____

Score _____

Skill Building: Two-Word Poem

Background for the Teacher

Definition: A two-word poem has just two words on each line and can be about any topic. For this lesson, the students will write a two-word poem about a parent, grandparent, aunt, or uncle.

Skills needed: No special skills are needed.

Materials needed: All About . . . (page 99), Photo Frame (page 100), Two-Word Poem Worksheet (page 101), Response and Assessment (page 105), A Request for Families (page 102), photos of the students' family members (the subjects of their poems), construction paper, glue, markers, scissors, and crayons

Preparation: Reproduce one copy of each worksheet for each student. Send the request letter home with students, explaining that they are to find a photograph of their poem's subject. Gather other materials for the lesson.

Lesson Plan

Pre-writing

1. When each student has created a drawing or brought in a photograph of a parent, grandparent, aunt, or uncle, have him or her place the photograph or drawing on his or her desk. Distribute copies of All About . . . to the students. Decide if the students can work on the task individually or with you in small groups.

2. Explain to students that they are to generate ideas about their topic people. Share the Student Samples of Two-Word Poems and discuss them.

3. Distribute copies of the Two-Word Poem Worksheet to students.

4. Instruct students to use the worksheet to plan their two-word poems. (You may assign a minimum and maximum number of lines according to your students' abilities.)

Drafting

1. Have the students complete the Two-Word Poem worksheet, using their All About . . . worksheets and their photographs or drawings. These may suffice as their first draft. If necessary, have students write an additional draft.

Skill-Building: Two-Word Poem *(cont.)*

Revising/Editing

1. When the poem is drafted, students should share their two-word poems with peer responders. Provide the Response and Assessment sheet for this purpose. Peer responders should check to make sure that the title of the poem is the name of a person, that each line contains only two words, and that every line adds to the description of the person.

2. After the students have had an opportunity to share and make suggestions, allow time for students to make any revisions they wish prior to writing a final copy.

Publishing

1. Have the students mount their final drafts and photos on construction paper. Encourage creative decoration—such as borders—for their work.

2. Create a special bulletin board display for an open house or some other activity that will bring many visitors.

Student Samples of Two-Word Poems

Grandpa

Gum chewing
Hug giving
Tickle tickler
Surprises always.

Aunt Sheila

Tall, dark
Blue eyes
Fair skin
Crinkled smile
Vanilla scented
Book reading
Tap-dancing
Coming soon.

Mama

Hugs me
Sings sweetly
Bakes cookies
Tucks in
Finds shoes
Loves me.

My Room

Tiny, blue
White bed
Books, desk
Windows, door
Closet, mirror
Wooden floor
Door closed,
Lights out,
Good night!

All About . . .

(Place photo or drawing here while you work.)

Answer the following questions about the person in your picture:

What is the name of the person in your picture?

_____

How do you know this person?

_____

What color hair does this person have?

_____

What color eyes does this person have?

_____

Is this person tall, short, or in-between?

_____

Is this person young, old, or in-between?

_____

What does this person do?

_____

What do you like to do with this person?

_____

What do you like best about this person?

_____

Photo Frame

Color the frame. Cut out the middle rectangles. Place the frame over your photos or drawings.

Two-Word Poem Worksheet

The topic for my two-word poem is: _____

1. Here are two words about who this person is to me (for example: loving grandmother, silly sister, best friend, etc.):

   _____

2. Here are four words that describe what this person looks like:

   _____

3. Here are four words that describe what this person does:

   _____

4. Here are four words that tell what I like to do with this person:

   _____

5. Here are four words that tell what I like about this person:

   _____

Directions: First, circle your two favorite words for numbers 2, 3, 4, and 5 above. Next, write your topic in the title space for the poem below. In the space for line number 1, write the two words you chose for number 1 above. In the space for line 2, write the two words you circled for number 2 above. For space 3, write the two words you chose to describe what the person does. Fill in space 4 with the two words you circled for number 4 above. And, finally, write the two words you chose for what you like about your person on line 5.

Title: _____

1. _____

2. _____

3. _____

4. _____

5. _____

Congratulations! You've written a two-word poem.

A Request for Families

Dear Family,

In our class, we will be learning how to write a poem about someone to whom we are close. Please help your child find a photograph or snapshot of a grandparent, aunt, uncle, parent, sibling, or good friend to bring to school. The photograph will be part of a display featuring the students' poems.

Please do not send a valuable and irreplaceable photograph. While every effort will be made to return the photograph to you, there is no guarantee, as the students will be working with the photos to inspire their writing. If you do not have a photograph, have your child create a drawing instead. We will need the photographs or drawings by _____.

Sincerely,

_____

Content Connections for Two-Word Poems

Social Studies

Choose a person from history. This may be someone from a list your teacher will give you or someone you choose. You will need to talk about this person in class with your teacher and look for some information about him or her. You will need to collect your information so you will have it when it's time to write. When you have enough information, write a 3- to 5-line two-word poem about this person. Use his or her name as the title of your poem.

Science

Think about your favorite season or type of weather. You may, for example, choose winter or rain. Brainstorm a list of words that describe your topic. What does it sound like, feel like, etc.? Why do you like it? Write a 3- to 5-line two-word poem about your topic.

Content Connections for Two-Word Poems *(cont.)*

Language Arts

Think of a character from a book you have recently read or heard. Write or dictate a list of all the things you can think of about the character: what he or she looks like, does, thinks, likes, etc. Circle your favorite words and write a 3- to 5-line two-word poem about the character. Write his or her name at the top for the title.

Fine Arts

Listen to a selection of classical music. Listen to it a second time, but this time make some notes about how it sounds to you. Does it sound peaceful, angry, fast, or slow? Does it remind you of the ocean, or birds, or elephants? Write as many words as you can about it. Circle your favorites and write a 3-line two-word poem about the music. Be sure to listen to the music while writing your poem.

Response and Assessment: Two-Word Poems

Author's Name _____

Poem Title _____

Responder's Name _____ Date _____

Responder:

Did the author . . .

❑ use the name of the person (subject) as the title of the poem?

❑ use only two words for each line?

❑ write only about the person who is the subject?

❑ use creativity and interesting words?

Do you have any suggestions that might make the poem better?

_____

Author:

Did you make any changes to make your poem better? _____

Were you creative? _____

What is your favorite part of the poem you wrote?_____

_____

What was the hardest part about writing a two-word poem?

_____

Would you like to write another two-word poem?   **Yes**   **No**

Teacher:

_____ Student used the correct format.

_____ Student grasped the concept.

_____ Student was creative and original.

_____ _____

Score _____

Skill-Building: Humorous Poem

Background for the Teacher

Definition: A humorous poem may be a limerick, a riddle, a joke, or just a poem that is silly. For this lesson, students will choose a topic and write a silly poem that is either rhymed or not rhymed.

Skills needed: a sense of humor

Materials needed: Student Samples of Silly Poems (page 108), More Silly Poems (page 109), Silly Poem Pre-Writing Worksheet (page 110), Silly Poem Frame (page 111), Response and Assessment (page 114), humorous photos and cartoons taken from magazines and newspapers, humorous songs on tape or CD, crayons, markers, glue, art paper

Preparation: Reproduce one copy of each worksheet for each student. Gather the pictures and cartoons. You may wish to mount and laminate them. Have a generous supply from which the students may choose. Locate one or more tapes of silly songs, such as "Five Little Monkeys," "The Ants Go Marching," "Be Kind to Your Web-Footed Friends," etc. Some sources are as follows: *Wee Sing Silly Songs* (Wee Sing) by Pamela Conn Beall and Susan Hagen Nipp (Price Stern Sloan, 1997); *Disney's Silly Songs* (Audio CD, Uni/Disney/Duplicate Numbers; ASIN: B000001M1F), *More Silly Songs* (Audio CD, Uni/Disney/Duplicate Numbers; ASIN: B0000061CP). Gather art materials.

Lesson Plan

Pre-writing

1. Begin by playing selections of silly songs for students. Have them listen to and become familiar enough with them to sing along. Discuss the silly songs with students. Which are their favorites? Why? If there is time, have the class create and sing their own silly songs.

2. Read aloud some silly nursery rhymes and other humorous children's poems. You may wish to try works by Shel Silverstein, Dr. Seuss, or Lewis Carroll.

Skill Building: Humorous Poem *(cont.)*

3. Distribute copies of Student Samples of Silly Poems and More Silly Poems. Discuss these poems and have students share what they like and don't like about them.

4. Tell students that they will be writing their own silly poems and have them brainstorm for topics, using the pictures and cartoons for inspiration. Set parameters according to your students' abilities (the number of lines, whether the poems should rhyme or not, etc.).

5. Distribute copies of Silly Poem Pre-writing Worksheet to students and have them fill them out individually, with partners, or in small groups.

Drafting

1. Check the students' worksheets (see if they have a topic and a workable idea), and then have them write a first draft.

Revising/Editing

1. When students have completed their first drafts, have them meet in small writers' workshop groups to share them.

2. Encourage students to offer positive feedback, to brainstorm together, and to giggle.

3. Instruct students to make any changes they feel will make their silly poems better, more clear, and funnier.

4. Distribute copies of Silly Poem Frame to students. Have them write or dictate their final versions on the frame. They may color the border, and, if you wish, mount their poems on construction paper.

Publishing

1. Collect the silly poems and bind them in a class poetry book.

2. Place the book in a writing center or class library.

3. Be sure to display the book at open house.

Student Samples of Silly Poems

I woke up and saw a bug,
It scooted under the rug.
It thought I didn't see it,
Until I went to free it,
By picking up the rug,
Away ran the bug,
It climbed into my shoe,
What was I to do?
I went barefooted!

On a hot, hot day,
I love a cold, cold ice cream
In a cone.
I count my money,
I walk three, hot blocks,
To the ice cream shop.
I look at and sample flavors
For about three hours
Until I choose
Double Fruity Toot-Tootie
And Chocolate Scream Dream
Then on the hot, hot sidewalk,
I take a lick and
Plop! No more ice cream for me.

My brother really bugs me,
I think he is a pest,
But when I left for school today,
He said he loves ME best!

More Silly Poems

Ode to a Flea

I think that I shall never see
A pest more sprightly than a flea.
A flea whose hungry mouth is pressed
Upon my shin! And I'll be blessed
If I can catch the horrid thing
Before he makes another sting.
A flea who does in summer dare
To sit on any skin that's bare
And eat his fill. If he should burst
To satisfy his fearful thirst
Then I'd be glad for one less flea
To hunt me out and dine on me.
A flea who looks for me all day
Then waves his fuzzy arms to say,
"Here, Comrades, is a meal divine,
Like juicy steak and heady wine."
If this goes on, I'll sell my dog
And buy a harmless pollywog.
Used with permission, Beatrice B. Beveridge
Van Schoonhoven, ©1940

At Home in My Finger Tree

I hurt my finger and you see,
It really, really bothers me.
I fixed it up as best I could,
And for a splint I used some wood.
It would have worked except, oh me,
The splint looked like a great big tree.
A bird, a squirrel, and one small cat,
A mouse, an owl, and sleepy bat,
A frog, a slug, and honeybee
Are cozy in my finger tree. . .
And THAT'S what REALLY bothers me.
Used with permission, Suzi Hardy, ©2000

Flying Popcorn

A piece of popcorn
Escaped from the pan
And flew across the kitchen
Like Superman.
It ping-ponged back and forth
Between the oven and the freezer.
Then it shot up to the ceiling
Like a daredevil trapeezer.
I tried and tried to catch it,
But it never missed a trick.
So finally I gave up
And ate a licorice stick.
Used with permission, Arden Davidson, ©1998

Silly Poem Pre-Writing Worksheet

My Silly Poem will be about: _____

_____

What I would like to say is: _____

_____

Here are some of my ideas to use in my poem (words, phrases, images):

_____

_____

Here is the very first copy of my Silly Poem:

Silly Poem Frame

_____

_____

_____

_____

_____

_____

_____

_____

_____

_____

_____

_____

Content Connections for Silly Poems

Math

What are your favorite numbers? Do any numbers look silly to you? Write a silly poem about numbers. You could pretend that they are alive and tell what they would do and how they would get along with each other. When you are finished, add up all the numbers in your poem and use the total as your title.

Science

Write a silly poem about a subject in science that you've been studying. It may be a poem about a bug or whales, or it may be a poem about the weather or flowers. Almost any subject can be used for a silly poem.

Content Connections for
Silly Poems *(cont.)*

Social Studies

Humor can be found in many places, even in social studies. Make a list of the people and events you have been studying in social studies. Think about them and choose one that might make a good topic for a silly poem. The poem doesn't need to be long, but it needs to include the important details.

Language Arts

Write a silly poem about your class. It may be about something funny that happened, your humorous twist on a classroom routine, or anything that you think is funny or silly. Gather all the classroom silly poems together in a class book or a poetry newsletter to send home to families.

Response and Assessment: Silly Poems

Author's Name _____

Poem Title _____

Responder's Name _____ Date _____

Responder:

Did the author . . .

❏ choose a good topic for a silly poem?

❏ use creativity and imagination?

Do you have any suggestions for making the poem better?

_____

_____

Author:

Before you wrote the final draft, did you make any changes to make your poem better? _____

Did you enjoy writing your silly poem? _____

What was the hardest part of writing a silly poem? _____

_____

What part do you like best? _____

_____

Would you like to write another silly poem?   **Yes**   **No**

Teacher:

_____ The student grasped the concept.

_____ The student made revisions that improved the poem.

_____ The student was creative and imaginative.

_____ The student made good use of words and vocabulary.

_____

Score _____

Skill Building: Descriptive Imagery in Free Verse

Background for the Teacher

Definition: Free verse is poetry that is not restricted to meters, patterns, or rhyme schemes. For this lesson, students will write free verse that is descriptive.

Skills needed: familiarity with the five senses and descriptive words

Materials needed: Student Samples of Free Verse (page 118); Thinking about Free Verse (page 119); My Free Verse (page 120); Response and Assessment (page 122); scenic photos from calendars, postcards, and magazines; tape recorder; art paper; glue; markers, crayons, etc.

Preparation: Gather pictures from calendars, postcards, and magazines. You may wish to mount the pictures on cardboard or construction paper and/or laminate them for durability. Gather the rest of the materials needed for the lesson.

Lesson Plan

Pre-writing

1. Begin by having the students meet as a class to discuss beautiful places they have visited.

2. Tape record one or two of the students' descriptions of what they saw. Encourage them to use as many of their five senses as possible.

3. Transcribe one or two descriptions on the blackboard or chart paper.

4. Discuss the descriptive imagery used. As a class, allow the students to revise, making the sentences even more descriptive if they wish.

Skill Building: Descriptive Imagery in Free Verse *(cont.)*

5. As a class, rewrite the description as a poem. For example, here is a student's description of the Grand Canyon:

The sun was setting and it looked like part of the sunset, except, instead of being in the sky, it went down deep into the earth! There were red and orange colors and even purple. It almost looked like someone painted it there, until I saw a bird fly down deep into the canyon with its noisy cry echoing. I could hear the wind moving through the canyon and smell pine needles. I will never forget the first time I saw that canyon at sunset.

Here is one way that the passage might be written in free verse:

> *The sun was setting and*
>
> *It looked like part of the sunset, except,*
>
> *Instead of being in the sky,*
>
> *It went down deep into the earth!*
>
> *There were red and orange colors,*
>
> *And even purple!*
>
> *It almost looked like*
>
> *Someone painted it there,*
>
> *Until I saw a bird*
>
> *Fly down deep into the canyon*
>
> *With its noisy cry echoing.*
>
> *I could hear the wind moving through the canyon,*
>
> *And smell pine needles.*
>
> *I will never forget*
>
> *The first time I saw that canyon*
>
> *At sunset.*

6. Tell students that free verse is descriptive. It often is similar to how we might describe things we notice with enthusiasm or awe.

7. Explain that free verse can be about any subject. Students can write free verse about a family member or friend, a feeling, or a favorite place (like a bed, playground, friend's backyard, etc.).

Skill Building: Descriptive Imagery in Free Verse *(cont.)*

8. Distribute copies of Student Samples of Free Verse and read them aloud. Discuss them together. What is the topic of each one? What do the students like or dislike about each free verse? How does the imagery help the reader to visualize what the poet saw?

Drafting

1. Distribute copies of Thinking About Free Verse to students. Depending on the capabilities of your students, have them experiment with free verse as individuals, with partners, or in small groups.

2. Meet to discuss the results in writers' workshop.

3. Have students work individually to complete My Free Verse. Take dictation from younger students.

4. Pass out the pictures to inspire students. They may choose one of the pictures as a topic, or they may choose a topic of their own.

Revising/Editing

1. When the poems are drafted, have the students meet in small groups to share them.

2. Encourage helpful suggestions.

3. Have students revise their poems as they wish.

Publishing

1. When students have their rough drafts, have them write copies of their free verse on art paper and illustrate them.

2. Hold a poetry reading with the students reading and showing their poems.

3. Create a class poetry book and share it with the school library.

Student Samples of Free Verse

The Blue Sea

We were all in the car like peas in a pod,
Snug and warm, some sleeping, some bored.
Around the winding mountain road the car went,
Taking us around and around.
Suddenly it looked like we'd fly into the sky
As if our car turned into an airplane.
Around we went and there was mountain only on one side.
On the other side, down below, was the ocean—
It went all the way to the sky!
We all woke up and looked so hard, we couldn't take our eyes off it.
It shimmered below us like a sheet of rippling blue
That went on forever.

The Bunny in the Field

I walked through the tall grass,
Green and moist.
I thought I heard a rustle,
I stopped, my heart pounding hard.
There was a rustle, and the grass was wiggling.
I froze.
Then out wiggled a tiny, brown bunny,
Crawling, hopping, its nose wiggling at me!

Grandpa Smells

Grandpa smells like after-shave lotion
And cinnamon candies and
The grass outside and
The wool of his sweater
And the leather of his shoes
And my kisses all over his be-whiskered face!

Thinking About Free Verse

Free verse
Is poetry without rhyme
And no form to hold you in.
You are set free to soar
And create snapshots and
Beautiful pictures to share.
Let your feelings flow
Freely, poetically, and meaningfully,
Perfect,
Just the way it is.

While you don't need to worry about rhyme or meter with free verse, it is important to think about expression. How do the words sound? Is there a flow? Use your senses and best descriptive words to make your free verse poem special. Try writing about the topics below.

Write a free verse poem about a member of your family.

_____

_____

_____

_____

Write a free verse poem about a favorite place.

_____

_____

_____

_____

My Free Verse

My topic is: _____

_____

Here is what I have to say (just write your thoughts and feelings here):

_____

_____

_____

_____

Here is how I have arranged what I want to say in a free verse poem:

_____

_____

_____

_____

_____

_____

_____

_____

_____

Content Connections in Free Verse

Social Studies

Choose a scene in history. You may look at a photograph or a drawing. Write or dictate a paragraph that describes what you see. Remember to use your five senses. Use your paragraph to write or dictate a free verse poem about your scene in history.

Language Arts

Write a free verse poem about someone you like, or someone who is special to you. Draw a picture of the person to go with your poem. If you can, give the poem to that person as a gift.

Response and Assessment: Free Verse

Author's Name _____

Poem Title _____

Responder's Name _____ Date _____

Responder:

Did the author . . .

❏ use descriptive words?

❏ use his or her senses?

What do you like best about the poem? _____

_____

Do you have any suggestions for making the poem better?

_____

Author:

Did you . . .

❏ make any changes in your poem to make it better?

❏ use as many of your senses as you could?

❏ use your imagination and creativity?

What was the hardest part about writing your free verse?

_____

What did you enjoy the most? _____

What is your favorite part of your poem? _____

Would you like to write another free verse poem?   **Yes**   **No**

Teacher:

_____ The student divided the lines in a logical, natural
            manner.

_____ The student used good descriptive words.

_____ The student used most or all of his or her five senses.

_____   _____

Score _____

Skill-Building: Writing the Stanza

Background for the Teacher

Definition: A stanza is to poetry what a paragraph is to prose. It is a unit within which there is a set and unified rhyme pattern. For the purposes of this lesson, the stanza that will be used is the double couplet with the second and fourth lines rhyming. The Roses-Are-Red format, which will be familiar to most students, will be used.

Skills needed: knowledge of rhyming and meter in poetry

Materials needed: Student Samples of Roses-Are-Red Poems (page 125), Roses-Are-Red Greetings (pages 126–127), Response and Assessment (page 130), scratch paper, colored paper, markers, crayons, pens, pencils

Preparation: Gather materials needed for the lesson.

Lesson Plan

Prewriting

1. Introduce students to the typical Roses-Are-Red format by reading some samples aloud to them (the Student Samples of Roses-Are-Red poems may be sufficient). Additional resources may include *Rose's Are Red, Violet's Are Blue: And Other Silly Poems* by Wallace Trip (Little, Brown & Company, 1999) and *Time to Rhyme: A Rhyming Dictionary* by Marvin Terban (Boyds Mills Press, 1997).

2. You may wish to write a couple of Roses-Are-Red poems on the board as a whole class activity. This will help students become familiar with both the process and the format.

3. Distribute copies of Student Samples of Roses-Are-Red Poems and initiate discussion among the students. What do they like and dislike about the poems?

4. Post a list of possible rhyming pairs that students may wish to use in their poems. Ideas to get you started appear on the following page.

Skill Building: Writing the Stanza *(cont.)*

Rhyming Pairs

blue/you	green/lean
red/said	blue/chew
yellow/mellow	yellow/fellow
green/mean	blue/clue
white/fight	navy/gravy
yellow/hello	white/sight
red/bread	blue/dew
pink/think	pink/stink
navy/wavy	red/fled
black/tack	blue/drew
red/fed	green/teen
teal/real	blue/flu
red/head	white/fright
blue/boo	green/seen

---

5. Distribute copies of the first part of Roses-Are-Red Greetings and scratch paper. Work with students in small groups to complete the activity.

Drafting

1. When students have completed the page and have confidence in their ability to write a Roses-Are-Red poem, distribute scratch paper so they can write a first draft of their own Roses-Are-Red poems.

Revising/Editing

1. Have students share their poems in small writers' groups for feedback. Encourage positive suggestions.
2. Have students write any revisions they wish and write a final draft.

Publishing

1. Distribute copies of the second part of the Roses-Are-Red Greetings activity (page 127), paper, markers, crayons, pens, and pencils.
2. In small groups, or with the whole class, follow the steps to make a greeting card.
3. Have students mail or distribute the cards to special people in their lives.

Student Samples of Roses-Are-Red Poems

Roses are red,
Violets are pink,
You are as sweet
As a lemonade drink.

Roses are yellow,
And daisies are white,
I hope we're still friends,
I didn't mean to fight.

Roses are red,
Violets are blue,
I made this rhyme
'Cause I like you!

Daisies are yellow,
Pansies are too,
They are both pretty,
And so are you.

Poppies are orange,
Dandelions are yellow,
I think that you're
A really great fellow!

Roses are red,
Violets are navy,
I think that your glasses
Just fell in the gravy!

Roses-Are-Red Greetings

You are going to make something for a favorite person: a poem on a greeting card. Begin with the traditional "Roses-Are-Red" poem and brainstorm as many variations as you can. Try finishing the poems below. Then, take another piece of paper and write some more.

Roses are red,
Violets are blue,
Believe it or not,
I made this for you!

Roses are red,
Violets are blue,

_____

_____

Roses are red,
Violets are blue,

_____

_____

In your poems, roses don't always need to be red, and violets don't have to be blue. Roses can be pink, striped yellow, white, or any color you wish. Violets can be purple, aqua, navy, blue-green, or lavender.

Example:

Roses are red,
Violets are navy,
Your hair is pretty
'Cause it's so wavy.

Roses are _____,

Violets are _____,

_____

_____

Keep trying. Choose one of your poems and write it on the front of a greeting card.

Roses-Are-Red Greetings *(cont.)*

To make a poetry greeting card you will need:

- one sheet of 9" x 11" (23 cm x 28 cm) paper (Light colors work best.)

- markers, crayons, pens, pencils

1. Fold your paper in half.

2. Fold it in half again.

3. Your card now has four surfaces (one front, one back, and two inside) on which to write and draw.

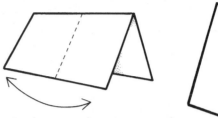

4. Look at your card, and decide which will be the front, the inside, and the back.

5. On the front of your card you will write the first two lines of your poem. On the inside of your card, write the last two lines of your poem.

Front	Inside

Roses are red,
Violets are blue,

Believe it or not,
I made this for you!

Happy Birthday, Grandpa!
    Love,
    Christopher

6. Add art and a personal message such as one of the following:

    Happy Anniversary, Mom and Dad   I Miss You!

    Love, Josette   Good Luck

7. On the back of your card, give yourself credit as poet and artist with a sentence such as, "Poem and art by the one and only _____."

                                                          your name

Extension: Plan ahead to decorate your card with dried rose petals. Place the petals between newspaper and press them beneath heavy books for 4–6 weeks. Fasten the petals to the card with a few drops of glue. Draw a stem using a marker or crayon. You can also create tissue-paper roses, tie them into a bouquet and attach your card to them to make a spectacular gift for someone special.

Content Connections for Writing the Stanza

Language Arts

Pretend that you are a character in a book that you have recently read. As that character, write a Roses-Are-Red poem that the character may write to another character or even to you. Draw a picture to go with it.

Social Studies

Choose a period or event in history. Brainstorm some topics and ideas about it. Write a 4-line rhyming poem about your topic. It doesn't need to be a Roses-Are-Red poem, but if you can think of one, go ahead and write it!

Content Connections for Writing the Stanza *(cont.)*

Math

Write the numbers 1 through 10 on a piece of paper. Now imagine that each number is a color. The number 5 might seem like it would be the color blue to you, and maybe the number 3 seems like the color red. Whatever color you think a number is, is fine. Now, write a Roses-Are-Red poem, only using numbers. Here is an example:

> Threes are red,
>
> Fives are blue,
>
> Subtract three from five,
>
> And you'll get two!

Science

Choose your favorite science topic such as lizards, birds, or caterpillars. Write a Roses-Are-Red poem about your topic. Here is an for example:

> Ladybugs are red,
>
> Blue jays are blue,
>
> Insects are crawly,
>
> And so are you!

Response and Assessment: Roses-Are-Red Poems

Author's Name _____

Poem Title _____

Responder's Name _____ Date _____

Responder:

Did the author . . .

❑ rhyme the second and fourth lines?

❑ use colors?

❑ use his or her creativity and imagination?

Did you enjoy the poem? _____

What suggestions do you have to improve the poem?_____

_____

Author:

Did you . . .

❑ make any changes in your poem to make it better?

❑ rhyme the second and last lines?

❑ enjoy writing your Roses-Are-Red poem?

What do you like best about your poem?_____

_____

What was the hardest part about writing your poem? _____

_____

Would you like to write another Roses-Are-Red poem?

Yes   **No**

Teacher:

_____ The student grasped the concept.

_____ The student wrote a 4-line stanza that rhymed at the ends of lines two and four.

_____ The student used originality and imagination.

_____ _____

Score _____

Skill Building: Onomatopoeia

Background for the Teacher

Definition: Onomatopoeia is a literary device that uses words that sound like objects or actions they are describing.

Materials needed: Onomatopoeia Poetry (page 133), Student Samples of Onomatopoeia Poetry (page 134), scratch paper, art paper, drawing materials

Preparation: Reproduce one copy of each worksheet for each student.

Lesson Plan

Prewriting

1. Introduce the topic to students by writing a few examples of onomatopoeia on the board. You may wish to create a poster with examples and illustrations to post in the classroom. Some words you may want to use include: *gulp, hiss, bang, slither, cough, meow, bark, slip, snore, hiccup, burp,* etc.

2. Read the examples aloud. Have the students read them aloud with you, or repeat after you.

3. Invite students to think of more examples of onomatopoeia by thinking of and describing sounds.

4. Define *onomatopoeia* for students.

5. Share examples of onomatopoeia from literature. Some interesting resources include the book *Little Dogs Say "Rough!"* by Rick Walton (Putnam, 2000) and "The Bells," a short story by Edgar Allan Poe. Try comic books, too.

6. Distribute copies of Onomatopeia Poetry to students.

7. Have the students do the activity in small groups or pairs. Provide assistance to younger students.

Skill Building: Onomatopoeia *(cont.)*

8. Distribute copies of Student Samples of Onomatopoeia Poetry to students. Read them aloud and allow students to try out the sounds themselves.

9. Brainstorm with students topics for onomatopoeia poems. Inform them that they can use any form of poetry they wish. Distribute scratch paper and have them each write a first draft poem.

Revising/Editing

1. Have students share their poems in small groups or with partners and make revisions.

Publishing

1. Distribute art paper and have students write or dictate their final copies of their onomatopoeia poems. Have them add art to illustrate their poems.

2. Create a bulletin board display to show off the poems and invite parents and other students to view them.

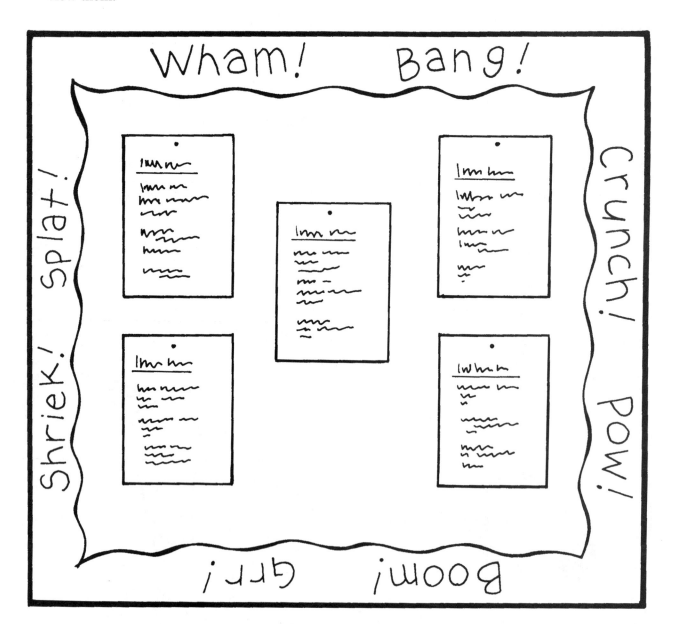

Onomatopoeia Poetry

Directions: Fill in the blanks with the sound that each item makes to create a poem about sounds. Be sure to add a sound title.

_____
Sound Title

_____ **Snapping** _____ bubble gum

Bubbles _____ **pop** _____

_____ teapot

Sausage _____

_____ bells

Roller skates _____

_____ kites

Balloons _____

_____ kids

Student Samples of Onomatopoeia Poetry

My Hungry Cat
I rub my cat's fur, swish, swish,
And she starts to purr, purrrr-purrrrr,
I purr and murmur to her in soft sounds,
Then she gets hungry and meows!

Summer Splashing
We splashed into the rippling, shimmering water,
We swam splashing, dripping, and spraying,
We got out and shivered
Then walked across the sizzling summer sidewalk.

Waking Up
First I hear birds chirping and fluttering,
Next I hear my brother snoring and snuffling,
Then I hear the alarm ringing and dingling,
Then I hear my brother banging and crashing,
Next I hear the water rushing and gushing,
And soon the breakfast sloshing and sizzling,
Then my mother humming and whispering,
Then my sheets rustling and my tummy grumbling.

My Mess
I dropped a ripe tomato,
It went splat!
The table fell upon it,
Squishing it flat!
I felt so sad,
I started to sob!
My mom then said,
"What's wrong, Bob?"

Content Connections for Onomatopoeia Poetry

Language Arts

Think of a disastrous thing that happened to you recently. Maybe you dropped your best drawing in a mud puddle, or fell off your bike and ripped your pants, or maybe you dropped a scoop of ice cream on the sidewalk (splat!). Write your topic at the top of the page, and then write all the onomatopoeia words you can think of that relate to your experience. When you finish, write an onomatopoeia poem about what happened to you.

Social Studies

Choose an event in history that could be described using onomatopoeia. You will want to choose something like a battle, a struggle, a march, or something active and noisy. Write a paragraph about the event. Go over your paragraph, adding onomatopoeia wherever you can. Using your paragraph, write an onomatopoeia poem about the event.

Response and Assessment: Onomatopoeia Poetry

Author's Name _____

Poem Title _____

Responder's Name _____ Date _____

Responder:

Did the author . . .

❏ use at least two sound words?

❏ use his or her creativity and imagination?

Did you enjoy reading or hearing his or her poem? _____

Do you have any suggestions for making the poem better?

_____

Author:

Did you . . .

❏ make any changes in your poem to make it better?

❏ use lots of sound words?

What part of your poem is your favorite? _____

_____

What was the hardest part about writing your onomatopoeia

poem?_____

Would you like to write another onomatopoeia poem?

Yes   **No**

Teacher:

_____ The student grasped the concept.

_____ The student used at least two forms of onomatopoeia.

_____ The student was imaginative and original.

_____ _____

Score _____

Creating a Poetry Publication

Background for the Teacher

Definition: A poetry publication, whether it be a newsletter, magazine, or collection, provides students with ongoing opportunities to write and publish their poetry.

Skills needed: the ability to write or dictate any kind of poetry or poetic expression. Illustrations are optional, but encouraged.

Materials needed: Poetry Magazine (page 139); writing and drawing paper; markers, colored pencils, or crayons; glue; poster board; storage such as file boxes; access to a photocopy machine, computer, scanner, printer, etc.; sample copies of literary magazines and publications (especially those geared to children)

Preparation: Gather materials needed for lesson and reproduce copies of worksheets.

Lesson Plan

Pre-writing

1. Introduce students to literary magazines by reading selections aloud and leaving copies in reading centers.

2. Instruct students about the workings of a literary magazine such as purpose, title, and function of editorial staff; frequency of publication; etc.

3. Discuss the value of such publications. Some points may include that they offer enjoyment to the reader, provide a place for writers to share their work, and publish material that might not otherwise be read.

4. Tell the students that they will be publishing their own poetry magazine, and they will decide, as a class, what it will be like.

5. Distribute copies of Poetry Magazine to students. They should dictate or write their own personal responses and then meet as a class to discuss the formation of a publication. If necessary, have students vote for their favorite choices.

Creating a Poetry Publication *(cont.)*

Drafting

Have each student choose his or her favorite form of poetry and write a poem for publication in the poetry magazine. Students may add illustrations, if they wish.

Revising/Editing

1. Have the students meet in small groups to discuss the poems they intend to submit for publication. Encourage helpful suggestions from peer responders.

2. After making revisions, the students will place their submissions in a file or box designated for the publication.

3. Have the current magazine staff meet to go over the submissions and their placement in the magazine. If they wish, they may return a poem to a student to rewrite so it is easier to read, or they may meet with the author if part of the poem is not clear.

Publishing

1. Using the format you have selected, the magazine staff will arrange and publish the pages of the poetry magazine, including one submission from each student in the class.

Additional Advice for the Teacher

1. Select, in advance, what form you will use in publishing the magazine, depending upon both the equipment available and the capabilities of your students.

2. You may select the first staff members yourself, and then rotate the positions so that each student will have an opportunity to serve on the magazine staff at least once.

3. Instead of a print magazine, you may wish to create a Web site publication.

4. If you are successful and your students agree, you may make your poetry magazine available to the entire school.

Poetry Magazine

With your classmates, you will be creating a poetry magazine. As a class, you will need to decide some things about your magazine.

- Will your magazine be published weekly, monthly, or every other week?

- Will it be given to your class alone, or will it also be given to other classes? Will students from other classes be allowed to contribute poems?

- How many poems and how many pages will be in each issue?

- Will you publish all types of poetry, or just certain ones? Will you accept illustrations?

- How will you produce your magazine? How often will you need to meet? How will the poems get into the magazine format?

- What kind of staff will you need for your magazine? Here are jobs you may want to assign:

Position	Duties
Editor-in-Chief	Supervises the production of the magazine
Managing Editor	Chooses the poems that will go into an issue
Assistant Editor	Helps with any editing and decisions
Layout Artist	Plans how the pages will look
Illustration Editor	Chooses the photos and drawings
Proofreader	Checks for mistakes before publication
Staff Artist	Does art, borders, lines, etc.
Production Manager	In charge of publishing the magazine
Production Assistants	Assists in printing, collating, folding, etc.
Distribution Manager	Distributes copies of the magazine
Distribution Assistant	Assists in distributing copies
Subscriptions	Keeps list of those who get copies

Creating a Poetry Collection

Wow! Give yourself a pat on the back! You have just completed some good, hard, and creative work during this poetry unit. You have written many different kinds of poems. You should have some favorite poems you'd like to share with others, and some that you may want to change to make them better.

To celebrate, here is one last activity. You will be choosing your favorite poems for a poetry collection all your own. Here is what you will need to do:

1. Choose your favorite poem from each kind that you wrote.

2. Put your poems in any kind of order you like.

3. When you have selected your poems and have the copies you wish to use, you will need to make a table of contents with the poem titles and page numbers. If you add any full pages of art, you will want to count those pages, too. Don't forget to think of a title for your poetry collection.

> **Table of Contents**
>
> My Best Friend
>
> The Horse
>
> A Funny Bunny

4. Next, you will need a Self-Evaluation form. This form will give you the opportunity to share your thoughts and feelings about your poetry collection. You won't need to list the evaluation in your table of contents.

5. Create a cover for your poetry collection. On the cover, you will need the title of your collection. (Some poets use the title of a poem for the title of a collection of poems). Be creative and artistic with your cover. You may want to draw a picture or just add some colorful designs. It's up to you!

6. When your poetry collection is complete, you may bind it into a book by using a folder or binder. Or you could punch holes along the left side and tie with yarn or ribbon. Your teacher will have suggestions and materials for you to use.

7. When all of the poetry collections are completed, it would be good to have a class poetry festival. You may share your collections with other classmates. You will also want to share them with other classes, your principal, and parents.

_____

Title

A Poetry Collection by

_____

Table of Contents

Type of Poem	Title of Poem	Page

Poetry Collection
Self-Evaluation

Author:_____

Title of Collection: _____

When you look through your collection, which poem do you
think you like the best of all?

_____

Why? _____

_____

Which poem do you think was the hardest one to write?

_____

Why? _____

_____

Which poem was the easiest for you to write?

_____

Why?

_____

_____

Now that you have a poetry collection that you wrote, how
do you feel?

_____

_____

Poetry Collection Peer Evaluation

Author:_____

Title of Collection: _____

Peer Evaluator: _____

Which poem in this collection do you like best?

_____

Why? _____

_____

_____

What things do you like about the whole collection?

_____

_____

_____

If there are illustrations, do they add to the enjoyment of the collection? Why?

_____

_____

_____

Do you have any ideas for your own poetry after seeing this collection? If, so, what?

_____

_____